TOPICS COVERED IN BECOMING A HIGH-IMPACT CANDIDATE

FORWARD:

- Why I wrote this book
- A bit about me
- What you'll gain from reading this book

SECTION I: FOUNDATIONS

- Closing the circle
- Practice, practice, practice
- You're on a mission—which one is it?
- Perfect jobs and perfect candidates?
- Corporate recruiting standards
- The impact of perception and bias
- Creating perceptions
- Why candidates fail on interviews
- The key players in recruiting process—what drives them?
- The importance of getting an offer
- Should you stay or should you go—drilling your own oil well
- "Career Time"

SECTION V: DECISION TIME

- Post-interview debrief
- Sending "Thank You" letters
- Using your recruiter effectively
- You've received an offer!
- How much time to make your decision?
- Considering counter-offers
- A bird in the hand—you have multiple offers
- Negotiating offers
- Accepting your offer
- If you've decided to reject your offer
- If you did not receive an offer
- A special postscript: Post Job Change Dissonance

CONCLUSION

FOREWORD

Having been involved in the business of recruitment since 1974, I have seen many a job market—the good, the bad and the ugly! For example, in the late 1990's the job market was wide open. If you were "in the hunt" during this time, between recruiters, the internet, print advertising and your personal network, you most likely had multiple opportunities from which to choose. Even if you weren't actively looking, you still had a regular stream of opportunities being presented to you. However, that phenomenon passed (and that's exactly what the boom years of 1993-2000 were—a phenomenon) to be replaced with an absolute crash in the job market in 2001-2003, which was in turn replaced with a more normalized market in 2003-2007. Midway through 2007, the job market tanked again, as has only been slowly "coming back" to again a more normalized market. Such is the cyclicality of the job market! But in any job market, whether boom or bust, every interview you take is vital! You can't afford to "blow off" or "trash" one interview because there will be 2-3 others out there just as good, if not better! There may not be! Your next interview might just be the only interview you receive that represents a quality opportunity. Because of this, it is essential that you are in a position to succeed on every interview you take. But, just how do you maximize your chances of success? How can you be the "best" candidate for every position for which you compete?

You'll note that I used quotations around the word "best". They are present for a very good reason. As you continue to read *Becoming a High Impact Candidate*, you'll very quickly come to the realization that in every competition it's being the best-prepared and best-informed candidate that will help you to succeed on every job interview you take. But wait, you say, why is preparation necessary? After all, despite what this guy Smith says, I know myself and my capabilities—there couldn't possibly be a better-qualified candidate than me . . . right?

To reference one of my personal favorites, Steven Covey (*7 Habits of Highly Effective People*), and putting "first things first", let's agree for the moment that preparation is essential to the success of any job search. As an example, you wouldn't expect a NFL coach to send his team onto the field for the Super Bowl (or any game for that matter!) without practicing first. He would make certain his team had done their homework. He would educate his team with regard to their opponent's past performances, their tendencies and their key players—even, if they can be expected to run "trick plays". The coach would also make certain his team practiced its own plays. He would ensure that his players rehearsed and rehearsed until they "got it right". In other words, the <u>successful</u> NFL coach makes certain that his team is very well prepared indeed, before taking the field. Even a team with superior physical ability and talent will <u>not</u> win consistently if they are not well prepared. To direct this analogy to our purposes, consider the following thought:

> Even though you may have superior functional job skills and better academic credentials when comparing yourself to other candidates <u>competing</u> for the same position, you can lose out to less qualified candidates consistently if you are not well prepared for the interview.

The converse is also true. We can find ourselves prevailing over "superior" candidates (i.e. better "paper" credentials, etc.) because of our thorough preparation and more complete understanding of the interview process.

WHY DID I WRITE THIS BOOK?

For over 30 years I have been intimately involved in the arena of professional recruiting—at all levels—from production roles to entry level to senior management positions. During that time, I have seen many candidates win the battle, that is, receive offers; and, many candidates who received poor outcomes. My goal is to enable every candidate reading this book to achieve a positive outcome in the game of interviewing. As an aside, even those candidates who "win" don't always achieve the positive outcome they are seeking. In many cases receiving and accepting an offer only leads to initiating another job search 12 months later when the candidate realizes that the decision they made to join the firm was not the correct decision after all. So, when I write that I want you to achieve a positive outcome, what I am really stating is that <u>I want you to be able to generate and accept offers from companies that will provide you with the best chance of achieving career success</u>. I have developed a methodology that when combined with the exercises, strategies and technique discussed in this book will help you achieve exactly that goal.

A BIT ABOUT ME

My experience in recruitment and selection extend over 30 years. It includes 12 years of corporate HR experience with high-visibility HR organizations such as Cardinal Health, PepsiCo, Inc., etc. and since 1987, in executive search and HR consulting. In 1987, I left Pepsi as Director of Staffing, and joined the nation's largest executive search firm specializing in Information Technology recruitment. After a successful year in New York City as an Associate (where I also won "Rookie of the Year" honors—the top performing associate from the 70+ hired that year), I was promoted and moved to Chicago to lead the firm's Chicago office. In 1989, I left that company and started my own firm, Smith, Scott&Associates specializing in Human Resources and Information Technology recruiting and Human Resources consulting.

Since 1991, I have taught Recruitment and Selection (among other courses) at DePaul University in their #4 ranked MBA program (*U.S. News and World Report's* "List of Top U.S. Universities and Colleges") as an adjunct professor. In 2005, I joined the University of Colorado's adjunct faculty in their undergraduate Business department as a Lecturer. Additionally, I have trained over 1,000 people in my corporate seminars.

WHAT YOU'LL GAIN FROM READING THIS BOOK

I've read more than a few books on interviewing and selection and scoured the Internet (job boards, career sites, etc.) to see what's out there in the way of current thought involving interviewing. I can state that I have not found another single source that provides the full scope of information that we're going to discuss in this book! Most "experts" seek to give candidates a long list of "do's and don'ts". That is, how to dress, how to write an effective resume and cover letter, which Internet sites to visit, even how to answer certain questions, etc. While these are important elements of a successful interview, they have been written about and discussed *ad nauseam*! We will not be discussing those issues in a traditional sense in this forum. Instead, we'll be focusing on the *tactics* and *strategy* of interviewing. We will discuss the complete interview process from beginning to end and develop an understanding of how to achieve your most effective level of interviewing performance. I am not going to labor over theory, but instead provide you with actual "tools" that you can practice and put into use in a real interview situation! You are going to get your money's worth in basic and advanced techniques that will increase your interviewing "batting average" significantly.

For example, in baseball, hitting 1 out of 3 – or .333 – will get you into the Hall of Fame. A well-qualified candidate will typically perform at this level. That is, for every 3 interviews taken, they will receive 1 job offer. However, as we've already discussed, in a tight job market—batting .333 is just not going to be good enough. I like my candidates to achieve a 70% success rate—i.e. for every 5 interviews taken, the candidate generates 3+ job offers. Of course, my "ideal" goal is to have you receive a job offer on every interview. But this is not realistic or in some cases not even advisable. Frankly, there are certain companies and environments in which we're better off not working. However, after over 30 years of recruiting experience at all levels, and across multiple industries and fields, I can tell you that succeeding 70% of the time is truly exceptional performance, and should net you most of the jobs you really want.

Before we start, I want to emphasize one thing . . . many of the ideas that are contained in this forum may force you to change your way of thinking about the interviewing process. These ideas will contradict the traditional manner in which most candidates prepare for and conduct themselves on interviews. I am also going to ask that you work <u>very</u> hard to prepare for your interview because my methodology requires that you "do the homework before you take the test". I realize that you might even feel that because you've had past success as a candidate, why do you need to change your game?

Consider the process of investing in the stock market. There are amateurs who make a lucky trade and make money—e.g. they invest in an internet stock and strike gold. However, more often than not, they fool themselves into thinking that their one success has made them experts and promptly lose their gains (and then some!) on their next trade. By contrast, professional investors find a way to win in any market, and win consistently! This is my goal for you. I recognize that you may be able to "luck into" a job offer for any number of reasons. But, I want you to win consistently in the game of interviewing; and not through luck or coincidence, but through design and intent. I want you to become a *professional* candidate—in other words, a *high-impact candidate*.

Remember, your goal should be to succeed 70%+ of the time, not the 30% ratio that even the most "qualified" candidates typically achieve. By reading this book you are benefiting from the experience gained in 15,000+ interviews and over 30 years in recruiting. What I've written in this book is a synthesis of the coaching I provide my own candidates before I send them out to do battle! In any head-to-head contest, my candidates invariably succeed—because of the preparation they commit themselves to before the interview.

In short . . . you've already paid for these ideas. Why not put them into practice?

SUMMARY

You'll find this book to be broken into five sections. Section I, *Foundations*, is designed to get you thinking about the underlying forces and "mindset" that shape the recruiting process. Section II, *Pre-Interview Preparation*, will help you prepare for your interview through a series of exercises and discussions. After completing these exercises, you will have a better understanding of your short and long-term career goals and very important, the company culture/environment best suited to your individual style. Section III consists of "Tools of the Interviewing Trade"—an opportunity to address a cross-section of interviewing problems and their solutions. Section IV, *The Interview*, will explore the interview in-depth and provide you with specific techniques and a question-answering methodology specifically designed to increase your interviewing batting average. Finally, Section V, *Decision Time*, will present strategies for the post-interview or "decision" period, including what to do after you've received an offer.

Before we start, please bear in mind that every candidate and every interview situation have the potential to offer unique challenges. No single book could possibly cover every contingency and variable that can occur in an employment interview. In other words, one size does not fit all. As a consequence, you may find it necessary to modify or adjust several concepts outlined in this book to best fit your own unique style and circumstances. As you read this book, I'd like you to picture yourself as an old-time prospector, mining for gold. Just like that prospector, you may have to move a ton of rock, but there will be definitely nuggets of gold contained in this book that will make your effort worthwhile.

Let's get to it!

*This book is dedicated to the 600+ people whom I
have placed over the past 25 years.
Working together has made us both successful!*

BECOMING A HIGH-IMPACT CANDIDATE

By Gary J. Smith

Managing Partner

Smith, Scott&Associates

SECTION I – FOUNDATIONS

THE MINDSET OF RECRUITING

CLOSING THE CIRCLE

We're going to start by conducting a quick thought experiment. It's called "Closing the Circle'. You're going to experience a very interesting phenomenon caused by the manner in which the human mind works.

O.K., let's perform our experiment. What I'd like you to do is to draw a circle on a sheet of paper, except leave a very small, but noticeable, portion of the circle undone. Then, stare intently at the circle for a full 60 seconds. Stare directly at it and don't look away. What I'm willing to bet has happened at the end of the 60 seconds, is that the break in the circle was completely filled in by your mind. In other words, you "saw" a complete, unbroken circle. Further, after 60 seconds, you can look away briefly and then look back to the figure, and still find the circle to be complete without a break.

You will find this experiment in most introductory psychology textbooks. What you've just experienced is the tendency of the human mind to drive itself to "completion"; i.e. to look for and formulate answers to problems, even if the solution is not immediately available. As a species, we human beings have survived and moved to the top of the food chain—not necessarily because of our physical prowess (if that was the case, lions and tigers and bears would be throwing peanuts into our cages at the zoo!), but because of this remarkable instrument we possess, the human mind. Our minds have made us great problem solvers. However, because we are inherently problem solvers, we are also unhappy with incompletion—and often, because of this unhappiness with incompletion, our mind helps us by "filling in the blanks". This very human tendency to fill in the blanks has been successfully proven time and again. In a study at Duke University (*Nature Neuroscience*, 8 April 2002) analyzing functional magnetic resonance imaging of blood flows in the prefrontal cortex, researchers found that the human brain automatically looks for patterns— real or assumed (more about "assuming" later!). This study found that the human brain will often create data so as to complete patterns—even where there are none. In other words, our brain has the ability to "fill in the blanks" when data is missing or incomplete. Michael Shermer, in his December, 2008 *Skeptic* article in Scientific American calls it, "Patternicity", or "tending to find meaningful patterns in meaningless noise". In many areas of our lives this trait can range from the innocuous to the necessary. But, consider when we are faced with an important decision coupled with incomplete data . . . this very human trait to "close the circle" can lead to erroneous and potentially costly decisions. In business, we're constantly being faced with having to make decisions based on incomplete data, only to receive *help* from this remarkable instrument—our brain. Our brains will often provide us with data that is not available empirically—but instead assumed or imagined and then, "close the circle" for us. But what if the data that our brain inserts in that empty space in the circle is not accurate? What can this do to the quality of our decision-making?

Another human trait closely related to "closing the circle" is our desire to be right about our decisions and choices—versus being wrong. This natural desire to be proven right has implications that can play out to your advantage in an interview situation.

Both of these traits can be critical elements in our success as candidates, if we understand them and allow them to work for us. To wit: when a company contacts us to come in for an interview, they are already predisposed to like us and hire us. Can you imagine a hiring manager saying to HR, "Well, this one looks like a loser, but let's bring him in anyway"? Not a chance! Companies do not waste time interviewing candidates who are not, at least on paper, qualified. When you receive the call to come in for an interview it is because the company felt that you have a good chance of being hired. When a resume is reviewed and a decision is made to bring a candidate in for an interview, the natural tendency of the company representative is initially to be positively disposed towards the candidate—sight unseen! In essence, we begin the interview process with the circle only slightly incomplete (as in the diagram). By applying the techniques of *Becoming a High-Impact Candidate*, we will work hard *to* create such strong perceptions and images that the company's interviewers will work mental overtime to "close the circle" and extend a job offer to us. By applying the *High-Impact* methodology, you'll find yourself receiving offers for positions—even though you are not the "perfect" candidate, and even though you may have a few glaring holes in your background that, under normal circumstances, could be disqualifying. After reading this book and applying the methodology described within it, you will prevail in the interview process because of the images that you are going to project and the perceptions you will create. You are going to be such a strong presence that a company's interviewers will be congratulating themselves for being so "right" about bringing you in for an interview, and then, being "right" about offering you a position. The concept of "closing the circle", then, is an important part of the foundation upon which we will build your interviewing success.

PRACTICE, PRACTICE, PRACTICE

As you read on, you'll note that I am somewhat of a maniac on the subject of preparation and practice, practice, practice. Don't forget an interview, like any other selling situation, is a performance. Being prepared and rehearsing for your interview will significantly increase the likelihood that you will perform at your highest level of effectiveness. People have often debated the importance of preparation and practice prior to interviews—after all, if you have great credentials then all you have to do is show up and be yourself! Right? I offer two illustrations to make my point:

Have you ever watched a major professional golf tournament, such as the PGA or Masters? To be a participant in either, you have to be a <u>proven</u> excellent golfer. No flukes are allowed as in Kevin Costner's portrayal of the U.S. Open, *Tin Cup*. You must be a consistently outstanding professional. In theory, any golfer in the field has a chance to win the tournament. However, what happens? The field is ultimately dominated by a small handful of competitors. And of this small group, the winner is typically the person who can handle the stress, pressure and scrutiny of "being in the hunt" the best. Even those golfers not in this final group are all excellent! Watch them play at your local club and you'd say they were unbeatable! However, in a high-profile tournament, the pressure of the competition can significantly impact their usual performance. The same is true for candidates in an interview situation. Even the most normally relaxed and poised individual can be "off his game" in an interview—due to the pressure of the moment. Have you ever wondered why Tiger Woods seems to be able to hit golf shot after golf shot perfectly? It's not because he necessarily has the best swing on the tour, or the best putting stroke, or the best short iron game, etc. Tiger wins because he is usually the most focused competitor and does not let external stimuli interfere with the job at hand. A case in point was a Masters Tournament several years ago. Midway through Saturday's 3rd round, it was apparent that it would be a showdown between David Duval and Tiger—two great champions! However, by the second hole of Sunday's final round, I knew that while Duval would contend, he was not going to win. You could see in his body language, the subtle effect that the pressure of going "head-to-head" with Tiger was having on him. The outcome was predictable. While Duval made a charge, he couldn't sustain his momentum, and began to fade. Tiger, by contrast, was relentless—he hit great shot after great shot, showing about the same reaction to pressure as if he were on a practice round. He knew he was going to win—he never doubted the outcome!

Example number two involves a segment of NBC News bi-weekly, *Dateline* (29 May 2001). In this report, 10 University of Nebraska students were asked to attempt 20, 5-foot putts as part of a psychology experiment. During the experiment they were "hooked up" to equipment that would monitor their heart rate and brain activity. The results of the first 20 putts were duly recorded and then used as a "baseline" of their performance. The equipment recorded their heart rate and the level and location of brain activity that resulted from their performance. They were then asked to complete a second round of 20 putts. To their surprise, just as they were starting their second round, the *Dateline* reporter came out of hiding and introduced himself—along with his camera crew—indicating that they would be taping the student's performance (on the second round of 20 putts) for airing on national television. Further, the reporter offered a $300.00 bonus if the students could beat their own performance in the first round!

The predictable happened. With the television cameras rolling and the pressure associated with being on national television, student performance plummeted! Heart rates increased from 70 beats per minute to over 140 per minute! Brain activity was significantly increased and was spread throughout the brain, instead of being localized— indicating a lack of focus! The result was that five students, who had sunk 12+ of their first 20 putts, couldn't even sink 5 putts on their second attempt. However, five other students were able to equal or better their performance with "the pressure on"! Care to guess, what everyone in that second group had in common?

While the five successful students also showed an increase in heart rate (although not as significant), all five showed brain activity that was more localized, indicating a greater ability to focus on the matter at hand. What the successful five had in common, was that they (both male and female) were also student-*athletes* (although non-golfers)! The conclusion drawn was that the student-athletes were more accustomed to operating in pressure situations (i.e., they had more *practice* in pressure situations) and as a result, could handle the pressure better and maintain a more consistent level of focus—and therefore performance—when the "heat was on".

What should these two illustrations mean to us? Simply, that for most of us, an employment interview is not an ordinary event in our lives. It is an unusual event. Attached to this unusual event is also a significant amount of pressure on us to perform well, to be liked, not to embarrass ourselves, etc. Right?

The method by which we can manage the inevitable pressure associated with interviewing is by being totally prepared and by practicing beforehand. Like the student athletes in the *Dateline* experiment, or Tiger Woods, we'll be in a better position to handle interview pressure and maintain our focus, through the application of pre-interview preparation and practice before the interview. It is this greater focus that will allow you to perform at your highest level of effectiveness.

Having now discussed the importance of thorough preparation, we need to *begin with the end in mind*—another "Coveyism". That is, identify the single, key objective upon which to focus so as to develop a successful interviewing strategy and create a high-impact interviewing presence. In other words, what is your mission on a job interview? Or, what is the most important thing you hope to accomplish on any job interview?

YOUR MISSION AS A CANDIDATE

A key element of strategy is to understand your objective or goal before you begin your mission—again referencing Covey, to "begin with the end in mind". Simply put, you have only one objective to achieve when you go out on an employment interview. That objective is to:

RECEIVE A JOB OFFER

Your objective is <u>not</u> to gather data or "fact find"; <u>not</u> to meet new people; <u>not</u> to sit back and decide "if you're going to like it" at the firm; etc. Your primary objective is to receive a job offer from <u>every</u> company that interviews you. I have known many candidates who have been rejected for jobs that would have been great career moves—jobs that they really wanted—because they did not express sufficient enthusiasm and interest to the hiring company by their manner, questions and body language during the interview. If you do not approach every interview with the intent of receiving an offer, then you are wasting everyone's time—most important, your own! Don't forget, you're the only one in the process who is <u>not</u> being paid for the time they spend during the interview process. Everyone else is being paid to sit and listen to you. In their minds, even if you're not the candidate, the company's interview team can at least console themselves by knowing that they are still being paid to be there. In your case, though, without an offer as an output for your time investment, you receive nothing and are squandering your limited and valuable time by being away from your job to go on meaningless interviews—not to mention the other potential "costs" of interviewing with another company while being employed. Therefore, your mission during a job interview is to create such a strong image, and present your skills and talents so effectively, that you receive a job offer for every position for which you interview. In short, if you're going to invest the time necessary to go to a company and interview, then . . . GO FOR IT! There will be plenty of time to decide whether you'll accept an offer, *after* you've received one. Certainly, it is understood that not every interview will involve a position or company that is exactly what you want. You may choose not to continue in the interview process after a first interview or to not accept an offer when it is made. However, to insure *consistent* success, it is very important that you perform *consistently* on every job interview.

Would it surprise you if I stated that most candidates accept offers for positions that do not meet their "ideal" criteria—or that most companies extend offers to candidates who likewise do not meet their "ideal"? This does not mean that either party is lowering their standards. What is taking place is that, as in life, the parties are attempting to achieve a balance between the ideal and practical reality. We find this to be true in our everyday life, too. Some level of reality-based *compromise* is the standard course of events in all human interaction.

PERFECT JOBS AND PERFECT CANDIDATES

How often do you get <u>exactly</u> what you want in a relationship? Think it over. Regarding relationships, either personal or professional—can a truly good relationship ever be achieved without both parties in the relationship striving to achieve balance through compromise? Of course, the answer to this question is "No", because life itself is very often a compromise. This is also true for the recruiting and hiring process, because with few exceptions, *there is no such thing as the perfect candidate . . . and, there is no such thing as a perfect company or job*. With every position filled, there are inevitably compromises made by both parties.

I've always told my corporate clients that if a candidate had "everything" (skills, experience, etc.) they were looking for, they had better be prepared to significantly increase the candidate's compensation. Without a significant increase in pay, why would a "perfect" candidate (i.e. one who has done everything that the new position requires) accept that firm's offer—barring other factors? There would be no growth opportunities for that individual—simply an opportunity to repeat their prior experience for the benefit of another company. Also, because firms tend to pay within a similar range for "like" positions, the increase in salary that candidates typically receive when changing companies is only marginally (8%-15%) better what they are earning with their current company. In fact, in many cases, the salary offered by the new firm represents a "lateral move" dollar-wise. As a result, money alone is never the long-term answer to making a good employment decision—by either party! The new role must offer something new to learn, a new challenge, or an opportunity for greater career growth. Without this added value, it will be only a short period of time before the candidate views their new job as repetitious and but a continuation of their previous position—with all of the attendant dissatisfactions that caused him to look in the first place. Therefore, beyond dollars, why would a candidate seek to join a new company and leave the security of their current role/company, unless they could get the opportunity to learn new skills or gain additional experience?

Despite this reality—which companies quickly comprehend as they progress through the recruiting process—most companies begin the process looking for the "perfect candidate". However, because that "perfect" person rarely, if ever, exists, companies, find themselves extending offers to candidates, who while not "perfect", come *closest* to their initial ideal.

Candidates often wonder, "If that's so, then what are companies really looking for?" Even with companies that state that they don't or won't compromise, the candidate ultimately hired can be markedly different from the specifications set at the beginning of the search. This is because the person hired represents the qualities and abilities that are actually *needed* for the position, not what was *wanted* at the outset. Rarely have I completed a search with someone who represents the "perfect candidate" at the outset of the search.   Remembering my earlier point, if the candidate was so perfect, why would they want the job? Therefore, never worry if you're not the perfect candidate.   By applying the proper interviewing methodology you'll find you can be successful in securing offers even when you're not entirely qualified, or perfect, for the position from a technical or functional perspective.

For example, a company may advertise for a candidate with 4 years of experience in a given skill (e.g. programming, taxation, circuit design, etc.).   What happens?   They eventually hire a candidate with 2 years of experience because the individual was exceptionally polished or because the "chemistry" with the hiring manager was great.   Referring to our earlier illustration, the company was able to "close the circle" with that candidate.

Candidates compromise in the same manner. I've had candidates who have accepted offers from firms 1½ commuting hours from home or no increase in pay, because the position offered outstanding opportunities for growth. This, despite the fact, that when we initially spoke they indicated that under no circumstances would they be willing to commute greater than 50 minutes from their home or accept less than a 20% increase in pay.

Seen in a broader perspective, as a candidate contemplating a job change, you should be prepared to evaluate the position and the company in the light of how accepting the offer will position you to do other jobs later in your career. That is, will this new position better prepare you to get to the level or into the role that you ultimately want? If it can, then maybe you may choose to sacrifice a few short-term goals to make a major gain longer term. You may not get everything on your initial wish list—but only you are in a position to decide where to compromise. For example, it's a terrific concept to search for a company with which you feel you can spend your entire career. However, the key word in the last sentence is "concept". The reality is that it is not likely that any company you join next will become the company from which you retire. You will make many job changes over the course of your career. Therefore, it is essential that you seriously consider how the job for which you are interviewing— even if it is not exactly what you want—will help prepare you for future roles in your career. If it can, then maybe a short-term compromise will net you huge longer-term benefits over the course of your working life.

Just to be clear—am I stating that you should "lower your standards" and accept just any offer that comes your way? ABSOLUTELY NOT! What I am stating is that you should go into every interview knowing that preparation and technique will create interview success for you (i.e. receiving an offer), even if you are not the perfect candidate on paper—because *there are no perfect candidates*! Just like Tiger Woods, I want you to go into every interview with the confidence that you will succeed—knowing that you have the ability to generate an offer from every company with which you meet

CORPORATE RECRUITING STANDARDS

All companies set different standards when making hiring decisions. Some companies hire based on the person's ability to do the job today, without regard to long-term "fit" within the firm's culture or the promotability of the candidate. Other companies will hire slightly (or even significantly) less qualified candidates from a functional or technical perspective initially, because they are focused on longer-term issues such as the candidate's able to learn and grow within the organization. My experience has been that the Human Resources function plays an increasingly impactful role in most successful companies. As a result, the more sophisticated a company is from a Human Resources point-of-view, the more emphasis is placed on qualities other than the candidate's immediate technical or functional skills. These qualities include the candidate's ability to communicate, potential for personal and professional growth, "chemistry" or fit (or how well the candidate meshes with the cultural norms of the firm) or other long-term concerns. However, here's a quick caveat: *beware any company that wants to hire you without paying attention to your fit within their culture*. You'll be able to smoke these companies out by the questions that they ask, or when you find them being willing to pay a significant premium—that is, substantially above the "market rate"—for your skills. These are quick tip-offs that their interest in you as a person is short-term—and instead focused on your ability to do a specific job (the one you will be hired to do) and not necessarily other (i.e. future) jobs within the company. What this means to you is that when your "utility" is finished at the firm (i.e. you've done the job needing to be done) you could be tossed aside and discarded if the firm hits a financial bump. Remember the "training wheels" that you used when first learning to ride a bike? They were important only long enough for you to gain balance and proficiency in riding—but once they served their purpose and were no longer needed, that were taken off and discarded—never to be used again. Consider the many people who joined dot.coms and other similar types of firms in the 90's—being lured with the promise of stock options, cash bonuses, etc.—and who were then laid-off when things got a bit tough or when the firm decided to "restructure" or "reorganize". It's fair to say that these companies were hiring people for the "here and now" (i.e. they were able to do the job that needed to be done at the moment!) vs. the long term. While this mindset may fit into *your* plans as well, always make certain that if you get serious about a company in this type of hiring mode, that you have an *escape hatch* (a means of exiting the company with newly gained skills) identified <u>before</u> you accept their offer. It is very flattering to be "wanted" and to be compensated handsomely, but please understand that a company's largess may come at a career price. When considering such a firm—or any firm for that matter—try to make certain that there is equity, or balance, between what you are *giving* and what you are *receiving* from an organization.

In many high-performing companies, by contrast, you may be hired, not because of your degree of immediate functional competence, but because you are seen as a great candidate in terms of your match with the firm's culture, or for your capacity to learn and grow within the organization. Joining these types of companies typically will prove most beneficial over the course of a career.

PERCEPTION AND BIAS

Often two candidates will be interviewed for the same position. They will have similar/identical "paper" credentials. However, one candidate is pronounced as the clear choice for the position and the other candidate, not even in the ballpark. Why?

This is a perfect example of perception vs. reality. Everyone has perceptions and biases. That's human nature. A classic example of how we are influenced by our perceptions occurs at the grocery store. As we walk down the soft drink aisle, we make a choice of cola beverages. One product has an advertising campaign that stresses tradition, the other product's campaign points out that it is the "choice of a new generation" and uses various pop culture celebrities in their advertising. Despite the fact the blind taste tests have proven that most consumers can't identify one cola beverage from another, when asked which they prefer, consumers will typically have a very pronounced choice. This choice is based, not so much on the quality of the product, as it is in the perceptions created by the advertising of the two companies.

An interesting aside, is that perceptions and biases become more pronounced the "closer" the product gets to the user. That is, items such as clothing, hairstyle, perfumes, foods, etc. are the most easily exploited and influenced by popular culture, peer pressure, advertising, etc., because they are physically very close to the user. Our biases and our ability to be influenced by our perceptions are at their greatest level for those items that are closest to us, or impact our feeling of personal success. Taking this into the realm of employment, consider that our personal success or failure is very much influenced by those we work with most closely. Therefore, as candidates, we need to be certain that we are creating the "correct" perceptions in the minds of our interviewers that will allow them to feel that they will achieve success if they hire us.

THE IMPORTANCE OF THE VISUAL IN CREATING PERCEPTIONS

This issue of perception forms the basis for the majority of literature on the art of interviewing. It is why so much attention is focused on proper dress and grooming and body language by many professionals in the field. However, to a large degree, the perception that your interviewer has of you is created from your resume and the first few minutes of your initial meeting. The old axiom, "You never get a second chance to make a first impression", is particularly true in the game of interviewing.

As an example, *The Executive Technique* is a terrific training program offered by a Chicago-based firm of the same name. Over a 2-day period, you are trained in the art of presenting; i.e., making an effective stand-up presentation before a group of people. *The Executive Technique* stresses (and has the research to back up!) that 85% of what we *retain* is based on what we *see*, rather than what we hear. This helps to explain why television is such a powerful medium in shaping our perceptions. For example, did a sick and haggard-looking Richard Nixon, in his infamous televised 1960 debate with JFK, create perceptions that cost him an election? To further support the importance of the visual, I often ask Human Resource professionals (who interview candidates daily) what they remember about a non-hired candidate, 2-3 months after their initial meeting. They will answer the question by describing the candidate's physical appearance or something that the candidate did on the interview (an event that was seen); or if they're really good HR types, they will reference where the candidate went to school or for which company they work (again, data that was **seen** on the resume). However, after 3 months, most find it difficult to articulate the candidate's functional skills or the reason/s for the candidate being rejected—unless they consult written notes. To be sure, the visual is key in creating perceptions—our eyes play the dominant role in creating our perceptions and biases.

Later, we will explore a methodology designed to create a positive and lasting first impression by giving our interviewers strong *visual* data upon which to form their perceptions about us as a candidate. But for now, let's review how perceptions and actual interview mistakes can cause "interview failure".

WHY CANDIDATES FAIL ON INTERVIEWS

I've always likened a candidate's chances on a job interview to be comparable to a soldier crossing a minefield. At any step in the process you can either innocently or with intent, get yourself into trouble. To illustrate this point, the following table represents a sampling of the reasons why companies have rejected candidates. After reading through this list, you're probably wondering how anyone gets hired! In all seriousness, as you read through this table, consider your own style and whether any of these reasons for the "boot" applies to you. Granted, this list is focused on college graduates vs. experienced professionals. However, in my experience, any of these reasons for rejection could apply to any candidate—regardless of level. Very often, knowing the reason for failure in advance can cause us to make corrections to our approach to the process. Our goal should be, through awareness, to minimize or eliminate any causes of interview failure.

Negative factors evaluated during the employment interview and which frequently lead to rejection of the applicant. As reported by 153 companies surveyed by

Frank S. Endicott, Director of Placement, Northwestern University.

1. Poor personal appearance.
2. Overbearing—overaggressive—conceited "superiority complex"—"know-it-all".
3. Inability to express themselves clearly—poor voice, diction, grammar.
4. Lack of planning for career—no purpose and goals.
5. Lack of interest and enthusiasm—passive, indifferent.
6. Lack of confidence and poise—nervousness— ill at ease.
7. Failure to participate in activities.
8. Overemphasis on money—interest only in best dollar offer.
9. Poor scholastic record—just got by.
10. Unwilling to start at the bottom—expects too much, too soon.
11. Makes excuses—evasiveness—hedges on unfavorable factors in record.
12. Lack of tact.
13. Lack of maturity.
14. Lack of courtesy—ill mannered.
15. Condemnation of past employers.

16. Lack of social understanding.
17. Marked dislike for schoolwork.
18. Lack of vitality
19. Fails to look interviewer in the eye.
20. Limp, fishy handshake.
21. Indecision.
22. Sloppy application blank.
23. Merely shopping around.
24. Wants job only for short time.
25. Little sense of humor.
26. Lack of knowledge of field of specialization.
27. No interest in company or industry.
28. Emphasis on who he knows.
29. Unwillingness to go where we send him/her.
30. Cynical.
31. Low moral standards.
32. Lazy.
33. Intolerant—strong prejudices.
34. Narrow interests.
35. Poor handling of personal finances.
36. No interest in community activities.
37. Inability to take criticism.
38. Lack of appreciation of the value of experience.
39. Radical ideas.
40. Late to interview without reason.
41. Never heard of company.

42. Failure to express appreciation for interviewer's time.
43. Asks no questions about the job.
44. High-pressure type personality.
45. Indefinite responses to questions.

THE KEY PLAYERS IN THE RECRUITING PROCESS AND WHAT DRIVES THEM

There are many people who influence the interview process and determine whether you will receive an offer. Of course, the most important person in a position to influence events is you! However, let's discuss the "other" key players and what drives their decisions about you as a candidate.

HUMAN RESOURCE PROFESSIONALS

Human Resource professionals can play a vital role in the recruiting process. Their responsibilities can range from simply identifying candidates to be brought in for interviews, to performing "screening" (either telephone or in-person) interviews, to administering in-depth assessment interviews that evaluate a candidate's functional experience, behaviors and fit within the company culture and long-range potential for career growth.

As indicated earlier, in many companies today, HR is playing a progressively more important role. However, you can't always expect that the HR professional who interviews you is an expert interviewer. In fact, the vast majority of HR professionals are not experts in the art of the interview—even though they perform the function regularly.

The reason for this is that many HR professionals see recruiting only as a necessary "punch in their ticket" to becoming a VP of Human Resources. Interviewing is seen as "low common denominator work" to be performed by the junior members of the team—even though recruitment and selection is the most important function that HR can perform! Don't think that HR is alone in how it assigns responsibilities! For example, in the Information Systems function, programming is at the core of everything for which the function is responsible. But yet, who are the programmers? The answer, of course, is that the programmers are the junior to mid-level members of the Information Systems department. Senior I/S managers are involved with "strategy", systems architecture, software evaluation and purchase, or long-range planning. They leave their programming days behind as they have move up the hierarchy of the Information Systems organization.

A key point to remember, then, is that very often you will be interviewed by someone who is still *learning* the art of interviewing. Like any job, it is during the learning phase that mistakes are most likely to be made. This may explain why we "couldn't get past HR"—even though we knew that we were qualified to go further in the process. Therefore, we may need to work very hard to help this often inexperienced, mistake-prone individual to make the right decision about us—that is, to send us forward to the hiring manager, and support our candidacy throughout the process.

Just to set the record straight, am I castigating Human Resources professionals for their interviewing skills (or lack thereof)? No, I am not. After all, I was "one" for 12 years! However, skilled interviewers are extremely rare in any function. You'll know when you've been interviewed by a "pro" only <u>after</u> the meeting ends! You'll walk away from the meeting, surprised at how much you "gave up" and how it didn't even feel like an interview. These are the signs of a truly skilled interviewer. However, trust me when I state that a skilled or expert interviewer is a very rare commodity indeed.

Another, important consideration is the very nature of the role of the Human Resources function in many companies. Truth be told, the "mission" of many HR professionals is to screen you out---not screen you in. Many HR professionals feel that the only way to justify their presence in the recruiting and decision-making process is to formulate the 9 reasons why a candidate shouldn't be hired, not the 29 reasons why they should. Hiring managers make the "yes" or hiring decision--HR professionals make the "no" decision in most companies. So, while the HR professional may sound friendly and engaging, they also have a mission—always bear this in mind.

"CONTRACT" RECRUITING CONSULTANTS

The widespread use of recruiting consultants or "contract recruiters" is a relatively new phenomenon. The process of replacing recruiters, who were employees of the company, with non-employee recruiters who are only contracted for a specified period of time, began in earnest, in the early 1990's. A Recruiting Consultant, although working on the company premises and working only for that firm, is not an employee of the company. Typically, they are paid by the hour and are either independent contractors or employed by the large staffing companies that have evolved over the past 20 years. In my opinion, trusting one your most critical functions—that is, the hiring of the very people who are responsible for the success or failure of the enterprise—to someone who has no real, long-term stake in the outcome, is analogous to turning over the deed to your home to a complete stranger and trusting him not to take the next flight to Las Vegas. A contract recruiter is driven by a totally different set of metrics than a recruiter who is an employee. A contractor is measured by how fast and how cheaply can they fill a position. By contrast, a recruiter that is employed by the company not only has these considerations, but also must be concerned about the longer-term issues associated with a hire—such as the actual on-the-job performance of the new hire, how well they "fit" with the firm's culture, and the long-term growth and stability of the individual. In other words, they have to live with what they've helped to create. A contractor, will most likely, not be around long enough to know whether or not someone they've helped to recruit will be successful. As a result, the very nature of how a contractor performs his job can be markedly different than that way an employee recruiter performs his. In my experience contractors are less knowledgeable about the firm, less committed to the long-term and more focused on the short-term; as in, "how fast can I fill this job and for what cost?" Also, you'll find that they don't have the "pull" with the hiring manager that most employee recruiters/HR professionals do. What this means to you is that if you're looking for a contractor to champion your cause with a hiring manager, you'll find that most just don't have the credibility to do so. Their role is viewed as simply to generate and screen resumes and arrange interviews—not to provide input into the hiring decision. By contrast, providing this type of input is at the core of the HR function's very reason for being.

A company using contract recruiters or recruiting consultants is not necessarily a bad thing—there are exceptions to every rule and these folks can be every bit as impactful as an effective corporate (employee) recruiter. However, it is another consideration that you as a candidate should factor into the process. If your company "contact" is a contract recruiter, they may not have the same influence on the process that a HR professional has. Plan and play accordingly.

HIRING MANAGERS

Hiring Managers are those individuals to whom you'll be reporting directly. They are the most involved and concerned individuals in the recruiting process because they know that their *own* success or failure depends on their making correct hiring decisions! They are usually most concerned about the level and quality of your functional skills. For example, if are you a software engineer, they want to know how well you know C++ or JAVA or Visual Basic. If you are a CFO, the hiring manager (usually the CEO/COO or Board of Directors) will want to know if you have had experience in M&A, have you performed due diligence, have you had experience in presenting to the financial community, press, etc. Hiring Managers tend to ask very direct questions and are concerned about your ability to function well in their departments and as a member of their immediate team. However, this concern can often create a short-term focus on the part of the Hiring Manager—that is, how can you help them today? By contrast, HR professionals and other senior executives to whom you will not be reporting, have the luxury of being focused on your long-term growth potential and fit within the company. As I indicated earlier, this difference in focus (short vs. long-term focus) can explain why individuals are often hired, only to leave within 12 months—as a result of being fired, unhappy, etc. They were hired based on their ability to do the job today, without any thought by the hiring manager as to whether they'd be a "fit"—even one year into the future.

POTENTIAL PEERS (COMPETITORS)

An important step in any intelligent employment decision is meeting your potential peer group. This group should be looked upon with close scrutiny and care. In this era of empowerment and team interviews, many candidates have been torpedoed by the unfavorable reviews of potential co-workers.

This group could look upon you as a competitor for future promotions or "face time" with the boss, or a cause of their needing to work overtime (training you!), or as someone who just doesn't like to party after work on Fridays. Their reasons for rejecting you as a candidate can be legion. As a result, despite the atmosphere of collegiality that conversations with peers often take on, you do not want to "let your guard down". Far from being your "buddies" in the process, they can sink your ship just as surely as a bad review from the hiring manager.

Actually, from a totally self-serving perspective, when you speak with potential peers, you should hold *them* up to close scrutiny. Are they the quality of people with whom you would want to associate? Can you learn from them? Would you want to "have a beer" with them? Pay attention to the type of people your potential peers are, because as your mom probably told you when you were 8 years old, "You are always judged by the quality of company you keep!" That is, in the future, people will form perceptions and make assumptions about you— sight unseen—based on the companies and people with whom you have chosen to align yourself.

PRESENT CO-WORKERS

Co-workers at your current job are on your side throughout the interview process. They want you to leave the company and further your career—even if that means they'll have to work additional hours to cover for your absence, or that the project you're involved with will stall until your replacement is found and that their careers will go into stall mode, too. They will be happy that you're moving on to a new opportunity with greater salary, stock options, and career prospects than they have. Right? This may sound too cynical, but I think you get my point. Many people see life as a "zero sum game"—that is, if you win, they lose. Personally, I'm a big believer in Steven Covey's principal (*The 7 Habits of Highly Effective People*) of *abundance mentality*. Abundance mentality speaks to the fact that resources and opportunities are abundant and that there is always enough to go around. Abundance mentality means that even if you win, I can win too!

Bear in mind, too, that there is always that well-meaning co-worker, who feels that it is his duty to you and the company to tell the Boss that you're looking outside the company—so that the Boss can attempt to "make things right" and that you will decide to stay. I think you know the likely outcome of that interaction. For these and many other reasons, my counsel is to not involve co-workers in your job search process, until you have an offer in hand. And then, put the high filters on the feedback you get. From a co-worker point-of-view you need to be discriminating when considering their comments and feedback—understanding that they too, may have a stake in the outcome of your search.

FAMILY

Your family loves you. They truly want what is best for you and the family. No cynicism here! However, a job offer that involves travel or long-hours (time away from home) or relocation (uprooting Junior during his senior year of high school), may not receive the kudos on the home front that you were expecting. My counsel in this instance is to listen to your family. Carefully weigh their concerns in your final decision. Remember, the ultimate decision is yours—but also remember that you'll have many jobs over the course of your career, but hopefully, only one family. Play the odds accordingly.

RECRUITERS

Because I am an executive recruiter, it would not be appropriate for me to attempt to convince you that all recruiters are wonderful people who perform a public service and work for the common good! Executive Recruiting, like any profession, has its good and bad practitioners. You'll quickly discern who is which as you work with a recruiter on a search. Questions that you'll want to answer when considering a recruiter include: Do they call you back promptly? Are they well informed about the market in general and their client in particular? Do they facilitate the process or do they get in the way? Are they reliable conduits back to the client company in matters such as salary negotiations? Do they still return your calls six months after you've rejected an offer through them or failed on an interview? My counsel is to have satisfactory answers to these types of questions before you decide to trust your career to a particular recruiter.

While we're on the subject of recruiters, this is a good time to dispel a long-standing, but totally inaccurate perception about recruiters. Many candidates feel that once they've given a recruiter their resume that the recruiter will go forth and begin contacting companies on their behalf. For the vast number of recruiters, nothing could be further from the truth! Calling companies individually and "pitching" candidates is a consuming and low-return use of a recruiter's time. The likelihood of generating an interview, let alone an offer, by committing the concentrated time to present you, is so small as to be *de minimis*—or so small as to not be worthy of note. Also, many recruiters (me included) are "retained" recruiters. This means that a company retains a recruiter exclusively to conduct a search for a particular role—a contract is signed, and money is paid to the recruiter up-front and in regular installments. The role of a retained executive search consultant is not one that lends itself nicely to "pitching" candidates. This type of recruiter may be willing to add your name to a conversation he or she is already having with their client, but forget about a retained recruiter calling multiple companies specifically on your behalf. He or she just won't do it.

Contingent recruiters, or those who receive payment only on the completion of a search, can be every bit as professional as retained recruiters.

However, by virtue of the type of work they do (again, a contingent recruiter only gets paid when they make a placement), the opportunity cost of presenting you to various companies on the phone vs. finding candidates for a hot job order can be prohibitive. A contingent recruiter might "blast" your resume to 10 or more of his clients via email with a cover letter and hope that at least one company "bites", but that will most likely be the extent of his efforts.

If a recruiter tells you a story different from this one, then either they're not very successful (too much time on their hands), or they're just not telling you the truth. Sorry to disappoint you if you thought differently on this subject.

As an aside, a quick word to the wise on resume "blasting". Your resume can be presented to 1000 companies—that's not a problem. It is only a problem if your resume is presented to the same company twice (or more) by multiple sources—or to your own company. When this happens 10 things can happen—9 are bad! My advice is to make certain you know where your resume is (and has been) at all times. Be assured that your resume is never released or presented by a recruiter without your express approval in advance. As I indicated, all kinds of bad things can happen if your resume is "in the wild" without your knowledge. Even posting your resume on a job board, such as Monster or Career Builder, is not without risk. Just be careful out there!

THE IMPORTANCE OF GETTING AN OFFER

Just to retrace our steps for a moment, I want to reemphasize that knowing <u>why</u> you are going on an interview is essential to achieving success. As I stated earlier, your primary goal is to receive a job offer. But you ask, "Why shouldn't I just go on the interview, listen, and wait until they sell me on the position?" All too often, candidates who take this approach tell this story:

> "When I first heard about the job from the recruiter, it sounded interesting and I felt I was well-qualified for the position. But even though I wasn't really looking, I thought, why not go on the interview just to see what was available in the market?

"During the interview I met four people. With the first two people I met, I just sat back and said to myself that they would have to sell me on why I should take the job. I'm sure I didn't appear very enthusiastic or present my experience as well as I could for them.

"However, by the time I met with the third interviewer, I was excited about the opportunity and could see the possibilities in the job and in the company. I could see how this job could help me from a career point-of-view. I was going to learn new skills and gain some great experience. From that point on, my enthusiasm showed on the interview and I knocked the socks off of the third and fourth interviewers I met. I was very well qualified and had the proven experience to do the job well! I walked out thinking that I had done well on the interview and would receive a job offer. I was excited.

"Two days later, my recruiter called me and indicated that the company had decided not to extend a job offer to me. I was surprised to hear this because I thought the interview had gone so well. The recruiter indicated that the company had informed him that I was 'too laid back' and that I had not appeared interested in the job or company.

"Apparently, the first two interviewers I met were key decision-makers in the hiring process. I had not impressed them with my interest level or my enthusiasm for the company. I was very disappointed . . . "

This, for someone in my business, is an all-too-familiar story. When I work with my candidates, I always stress the importance of getting the offer first and *then* deciding whether the job and company are for you. The reason for this is . . . *UNTIL YOU GET A JOB OFFER, YOU REALLY DON'T HAVE ANYTHING TO DECIDE!* Therefore, if you're going to take the time to go on an interview, then take the time to "go for it!" Show your excellent preparation and enthusiasm. Get the company excited about having you on their team. However, if ultimately the job is offered to you and you're not convinced that it is in your best interest to accept, then reject the offer with class and don't look back. But, don't forget—by performing well on an interview, you cause people to remember you positively. Today, no one stays with a firm forever. Who is to say that the interviewer who thought you were great, but that you rejected, might not have an even better possibility for you in the future—with that company or with the next company he or she joins. People have long memories for both talent and ineptitude. Make them remember you in the most positive of all lights. Remember, too, it is human nature to want what we can't have—even more. If you've been a great candidate, even saying "No thanks" (with class!) can cause people to want you even more in the future. Therefore, always work hard to be considered a great candidate, regardless of the initial outcome, as it can work wonders for your career over the course of time.

THE BIG QUESTION—SHOULD YOU STAY OR SHOULD YOU GO?— DRILLING YOUR OWN OIL WELL

Even as we discuss the importance of getting an offer, perhaps we should focus on an even more fundamental issue—and certainly among the most important questions that you'll ask yourself—*should you leave your company or should you stay*? The decision to stay with a firm or to look outside is a decision that to some people comes very easily, but for others, is a source of great mental angst. When I get into a serious discussion with a candidate in this area,

I always challenge them on *why* they would leave their firm. That is, have they investigated what opportunities are available within their current company to grow and gain additional experience? Believe it or not, it is in my best interest to challenge candidates on this issue— even if that means they decide to stay with their companies and I miss out on placing them in the short-term. Why is this?

When I work with a candidate during a search, I want to be very confident that they have done their homework in advance and have thought through the ramifications of leaving their company. It doesn't help my client or me if we bring a candidate to the altar, only to have them change their minds about leaving their company just before they say, "I do!" I never get upset when a candidate rejects their offer. This is a very important and personal decision—and not mine to make. I do get concerned, however, when I find that a candidate hasn't thought through the impact of leaving their company in advance (doing their homework) and decides to remain with their firm—even after they've already invested 10+ hours of interview time and have received an offer. That's a lot of everyone's (including the candidate's) time to spend only to reject an offer for a role that they should have known much earlier in the process was not right for them. A rejection of a job offer at that point by a candidate who has not done their homework, is analogous to a runner returning a football kickoff 99 yards only to choose to down the ball 6 inches from the goal line! In truth, that decision should have been made long before the interview process started, or after the first meeting. As a consequence, I always ask my candidates to do serious thinking about the impact of leaving their current company before we start on our merry way. The exercises provided you in the next section will help you complete this thought process and be in a position to assess the viability of an opportunity in real-time.

To put the impact of leaving your company into perspective, if you've been with your company for two years, then you have already made a two-year "career time" investment in the company, your immediate work group, friends, projects, etc. Most important, during this time you have established credibility within your firm. After two years you are looked upon as a source of knowledge and expertise. When your phone rings, it's really for you, not a wrong number! You have been with the firm long enough to get things done in the most efficient manner. People know you and your capability! For good or evil, you have established a reputation at your firm. Also, the "clock has been ticking" with regard to your next move within the company—after two years in the same job, you may be finally ready to make another move within the firm. Making a job change to another company could mean that you'll have to start all over again—reestablishing your credibility and re-starting your "career time" clock. So again, the question is: <u>should you stay or should you go?</u>

An analogy that my candidates have found helpful over the years is one that occurred to me in the 1970's, while I was a Recruiter for Pullman, Incorporated (a builder of rail cars, oil refineries and petrochemical plants among other things) in Houston, Texas. I call it my "Oil Well Analogy". If you relate this analogy of oil drilling to your career, you'll find that the decision to "stay or go" becomes easier to sort out. Let's consider the process whereby oil is discovered, drilled and exploited. To wit:

> When oil companies seek to find new oil sources, they do their homework first. The oil company's exploration unit will thoroughly investigate possible sites before drilling. They will analyze a region's past geological history, utilize satellite imagery for likely sites and when they've found a

likely candidate, they will perform seismic work to determine if there might be "something down there." If the seismic work comes back favorably, then the company will drill a "test hole" to determine if there is sufficient pressure, oil/gas quality, etc. to justify a production rig. Assuming that the findings are still positive, they will then drop a rig over the hole and begin to pump. And they will pump and pump and pump until such time as one of two events occurs:

First, when the well pressure drops and oil becomes more difficult to extract, they will often go to heroic measures—provided that there is still a sufficient known supply of oil in the ground. The company will inject steam to break up oil pockets or even pump salt water into the hole to cause the level of the well to rise (remember, oil is lighter than water causing it to "float" to the top) and thereby making the oil easier to extract. However, these measures have to be carefully considered as they are expensive and add to the cost of producing the oil.

Second, and key to our discussion, is that even if the oil company has to go to heroic measures, they will continue to pump the well as long as they can *profitably* bring oil to the surface. As the market price drops relative to the cost of drilling, the firm reaches, in economic terms, the *point of diminishing returns*, where the profit obtained in drilling becomes smaller and smaller until it finally reaches the break-even point. The moment the market price of oil drops below the cost of bringing it to the surface, the company makes an economic decision. It caps the hole, picks up the rig and moves on—even though there is <u>still</u> oil in the ground! They don't attempt to extract every last drop because they know that they cannot *profitably* bring it to the surface. So, again . . . even though there is still more oil remaining to be pumped, they cap up the hole and move on!

I think you can begin to see the connection between the question "stay or go" and our oil well analogy. Often, candidates will agonize over leaving their firms because there is still "more to be done." They lull themselves into a false sense of security thinking that their present company "needs them" and won't survive without their presence. Without their presence, the next 104 projects simply will not happen! However, this is just the candidate's ego and inertia talking! The simple fact is that there is <u>always</u> something more to do at any company—just as there is always some residual oil left in a well! The question that should be asked by a candidate is: *By staying, am I adding real value to my career in the form of additional marketable experiences*? Or, am I just repeating the same tasks for a third or fourth time; or performing a simple "variation on a theme"? In other words, have you begun, like our oil-drilling friends, to reach the point of diminishing returns on your *career time* investment at your current firm? Or, more pointedly, have you reached a juncture with your current company, where you can no longer earn a "profit" (in the form of new skills and marketable experiences) on your *career time* investment? Has it even become a losing proposition? If this is the case, then the smart call is to cap the hole, pick up your rig and move on to the next field (company) where you can profitably drill. Again, you'll want to do this, even though there is still "more to do" at your current company.

However, if upon reflection, you feel that there are still significant additional benefits (in the form of new skills, training, responsibilities, growth, etc.) for you to accrue by remaining with your current company, then you should stick around and continue to "pump"!

I only ask that you be smart about this. Think through your options before entering into the job search game. It will help you to better compare what a prospective company is offering versus your current situation and remove much of the mental agony that is associated with job changing, as in, "Am I doing the right thing?" or, "There's still more for me to do here, I feel bad about leaving!"

"CAREER TIME"

Because I've used the term *career time* frequently, it will be helpful to define what is meant by *career time*. It is a very important concept to understand. But first a caveat:

I know, in advance, that what I'm about to say is going to upset some of my readers. So be it! This book is not a forum for making you "feel good", but instead to encourage you to really think about your career and to focus on an essential task you will need to complete to achieve your goals—that is, developing a career strategy and plan. Doing so and working towards that plan will help to assure that the offers you accept and the companies for whom you choose to work, will be in alignment with your long-term goals.

Simply put, career time refers to the length of our *growth-oriented* working careers, that is, the number of years we will work until we reach our "end job/level". Assuming that most people will work until age 65, you would suppose that the average person has approximately 45 years of career time—a very long time indeed! However, this is *not* the case. When I use the term career time, I refer to the years spent with your career in _growth_ mode; that is, while you are still advancing in level, responsibilities and making significant gains in compensation. For most people, this equates to approximately 30 years. What this means is that by the time an individual reaches his or her mid-50's, they have most likely reached a career plateau—or are very close to it with the next and final move clearly in sight. For example, if you are a Vice President of Human Resources at age 55, then likely, you will continue at the Vice President level until retirement. You may work at several companies between age 55 and retirement, but again, most probably at the VP level. On a personal level, most individuals know where they're heading by the time they reach this age. By our mid-50's, we know our capability and the level to which we aspire; and we know if we have a realistic chance of reaching that

level.   However, even more important than our
perceptions, are the perceptions of others; i.e. those
who make decisions about us and about our capability.
It is those perceptions that are the most difficult to
shake and avoid.   For example, if you've been an
Information Systems Project Manager for the past 10
years and are now 55 years old, it's not likely that the
next company you interview with is going to consider
you for a CIO role. This may seem harsh, but it is the
way the "system" works. Your intended company is
going to ask the obvious question, "How can this guy
be good enough to be a CIO at our company, when his
own company hasn't recognized that ability?" Or, "Why
has he not moved forward in his own company? What
do they know about him that has prevented him from
moving beyond his current level?" Again, harsh as
these statements may seem, most recruiters and hiring
managers have the perception that by the time an
individual reaches their mid-50's, the "die is cast"
career-wise. Whether this is true or not is irrelevant—
because we are dealing with human perception. When
you attempt to change a human being's perceptions
you're taking on the toughest obstacle of all. Even a
heavy payload of facts cannot dent most perceptions
and biases. As an example, just consider trying to
convince a liberal democrat that the cause of

conservative republicanism is the right path—or vice versa!

Thus, it is the limited duration of career time that causes me to go a bit wild when I see people squandering their talents and their precious career time on dumb career moves. For example, consider a person, who moves from job to job without a plan—who makes 4 moves (different companies) in 5 years; and in those 5 years has moved laterally or only slightly forward level-wise. That person has burned up 20% of their career time with no appreciable gain! More often than not, they have moved for a slightly better salary, or a shorter commute, or because they were "bored" in their previous assignment, or because of the "promise" of stock options from the next employer. But the reality is that every time you move, you temporarily put your career clock "on hold" until you have re-established your credibility in the new organization. Your next job change must be calculated to move you forward level-wise, or provide you with a lateral move that is targeted to advance your career over the longer term. If not, then you have effectively wasted irreplaceable career time by making an unnecessary job change.

So, there is no misunderstanding, let me point out that there are exceptions to what I've just written. Entrepreneurs can achieve success at any age! A classic example is (Colonel) Harland Sanders. Sanders was 65 years old, decidedly unsuccessful and collecting $105 per month in Social Security when he created Kentucky Fried Chicken. Individuals at any age can defy past practice and perception and achieve success. Remember, Ronald Reagan was elected President of the United States at age 70! I do not consider 55 to be a magic age where all growth stops. Quite the contrary, with the aging of our population, people will have successful careers well into their 60's and even 70's and beyond! However, in writing this I am not considering "exceptions to the rule", but instead the majority of the workforce and the perceptions that most people have. And, if you feel I'm being "ageist", guess again—at my current age of 62, 65 is looking pretty young to me! I am simply trying to drive home the point that the time we have available to build our careers is very limited. We can't afford to waste career time by making job moves that don't advance our career plan. I want everyone reading this book to be successful—that is my goal for you—and if you're successful, I'll sell more books! However, to achieve success, you must have a career plan. You must have thought through your goals and how you intend to achieve them. To do otherwise, is strictly relying on chance and luck—O.K. for Las Vegas, but very risky for a career.

So, exactly how do we develop our all-important career plan? How do we better understand our goals? How do we identify what has made us successful in the past or what has caused us to fail? Can we describe the types of companies that are most likely to help us achieve the success that we desire?

In Section II, we'll discuss a methodology that will help you create this all-important career plan and coincidentally, make you a more effective and impactful candidate on your next interview.

SECTION II -- PRE-INTERVIEW PREPARATION

I'll bet you'd like me to tell you that all a great candidate has to do is to show up for the interview and get hired because they're just so great. Well, I'm not going to tell you that—because nothing could be further from reality. It boggles the mind that some individuals will prepare for weeks to make a 1-hour presentation to their boss or an executive committee so that they will be able to present and sell their ideas effectively and obtain funding for a new project—and, will proceed to spend literally zero time preparing to present and sell themselves effectively on an employment interview! The primary reason for this seems to be that most of us feel as though we already know ourselves so well that preparation in unnecessary. These same individuals enter the cauldron of the interview and find that they are totally unprepared to compete when faced with the elevated pressure present in every employment interview! They realize, too late, that they are unable to answer either fundamental or complex questions related to what they *know* so well . . . themselves. And, when they receive an unfavorable outcome, there is invariably disappointment and even surprise. The reality is that their failure was a direct result of inadequate pre-interview preparation. To succeed at a high rate (our 70%+ goal) you must create the right perceptions in the minds of your interviewers. To achieve this success under pressure and in a highly competitive job market, requires that you as a candidate be very well prepared indeed. Preparation relates to: A:) understanding your own goals and career objectives in light of your past experience, and B:) understanding your prospective company in the context of its "culture", financial and operational performance, and the likelihood that they will be able to meet your career growth objectives. In other words, to be able to intelligently discuss these issues (and more!), you'll need to <u>do your homework before you take the test</u>.

We begin our pre-interview preparation by discussing the importance of *knowing* your resume. In this next section, you'll not only get to know your resume better, but you'll also learn how to build a different type of resume than the type you most likely are now using. When you have completed this exercise, you'll find that your new resume will not only generate a greater number of interviews, but will be the type of document that will help you to control the direction and tone of the interview—by allowing you to focus on your strengths!

If you're ready, let's begin!

HAVE YOU HUGGED YOUR RESUME TODAY?

This may seem an unnecessary question to ask, but . . . have you studied your resume recently? Actually, it's a very good question to ask! You'd be surprised by how many candidates truly don't know what is contained within their resumes. Frankly, the interview is the wrong place to be getting to know your resume better, but it happens to candidates every day. For example, I've had candidates express shock at the types of questions I am able to ask simply by reading their resume. They're surprised that their resume "revealed" so much about them based on what was written, and sometimes, more important, by what was not. With the advent of outplacement firms, many candidates do not personally prepare their own resumes—the outplacement firm does. Unfortunately, this may result in the candidate only scanning their "professionally" prepared resume before it is sent out to 4,000 companies. Even candidates who write their own resumes will often forget what they have written, or fall prey to their own poor editing or proofreading. For example, just this morning I received a resume from a candidate indicating that her dates of employment with her current employer were "2005-2013"—inferring that she had <u>left</u> the firm. When I called her, and asked if she had left her company (she had given me no indication of leaving when I had spoken with her in her office earlier in the week) she indicated that she hadn't. I then pointed out the dates on her resume and she immediately saw her error. What she meant to type was "2005-present". Had she sent this version of her resume out to an employer, it could have formed the basis for rejecting her, sight unseen, based on the "fact" that she was "unemployed". Believe it or not, even today, there are still companies who are reluctant to interview candidates who are unemployed. So, beyond the obvious, why is "knowing" your resume a topic for discussion? Why is it important to know your resume well?

First, you'll need to consider the types of questions that could be asked from reading your resume and then ask yourself what areas of concern an interviewer might have based on having done so. Are the dates of employment synchronous? Are there "gaps" (periods of unemployment) that need to be explained? Are there a series of lateral moves or "backwards progression" (moving backwards in level or title) that may generate questions or concern? Does your resume identify key accomplishments that you'll want to make certain get discussed during the interview? I think you get the picture!

To help you perform this analysis, place yourself in the position of the interviewer and read your resume objectively. Ask yourself the tough questions that your interviewer is sure to ask you—or worse, not ask you and *assume* an answer! If this seems like a waste of time, remember, that your interviewers are going to be performing this same exercise before they meet you, whether formally or on an ad-hoc basis. The homework that your interviewer is sure to do can put you at a disadvantage if you're not prepared. By performing this self-analysis on your own resume, you can help eliminate being surprised by the interviewer who is able to identify inconsistencies. Unfortunately, being surprised on an interview can create defensive behavior in certain candidates—which is the kiss of death in the recruiting process. It can also make the candidate appear sloppy or lacking professionalism. The good news, though, is that by knowing your own resume well, you will be in a better position to control the flow of the meeting.

In the next section, I'm going to give you an exercise to complete involving your resume. This exercise will not only enable you to "know" your resume, but also generate two additional benefits that will move you into the ranks of High-Impact Candidates. They are:

1. You will be able to transform your resume from a descriptive, but passive document, into an action-oriented selling tool filled with results and deliverables.

2. By completing this exercise you will, by default, become well prepared to respond to your interviewer's questions, and to demonstrate the contribution and impact you can have on his or her business.

Later, when we discuss "The 5 Questions", the importance of having done this preparation in advance of the interview will be readily apparent.

DEVELOPING AN ACTION-ORIENTED RESUME

Before we start, let me state that this section is NOT meant to cover every aspect of resume writing. You could fill a small bookstore with the books already written that purport to do this. I have a much narrower focus in mind that is critical to developing a resume that will not only get you in the door, but also facilitate your success in the actual interview. Our goal is to tackle your resume's *content* and the *message* that it sends to its readers.

Over the years I have reviewed literally tens of thousands of resumes. Some have been memorable—either as being excellent selling tools or as being just plain awful. However, the vast majority lie in the great middle—very much alike and after a day or two, totally forgotten by their reader. I'm certain that you are not surprised when I describe your resume as a *selling tool* because that is exactly what it is. A resume is NOT meant to be an autobiography or an epistle on your life and times. A resume has only two purposes:

1. To generate sufficient interest in your background that companies are motivated to invite you in for a personal interview. In other words, to pick up the phone and call you! Your resume is a "selling" document.

2. To set you up for success on your interview by providing your interviewer a path to follow in his initial line of questioning; i.e. during that critical first 10-15 minutes when he is beginning to "close the circle. This is a path that will allow you to emphasize your strengths and accomplishments.

Unfortunately, candidates tend to include too much and often the wrong type of information in their resumes. The result is that when viewed in a pile of 100+ resumes (about the average response generated from your typical *Monster* or *CareerBuilder* posting), or being scanned on a computer monitor, there are no instant "pick me" qualities evident. There is nothing to make that resume "jump out" of the stack. Consider for a moment, that most resumes today are viewed on the standard, corporate-issue 17" computer monitor, or even smaller screen laptop or mobile device. Multiple page treatises are just NOT going to be read—given the time available to the recruiter. Unless there is something compelling within the **top 2/3rds of the first page** to encourage the screener to read on—they won't. What do I mean by the "top 2/3rds"? Picture in your mind how much of your resume will appear on a laptop's full-screen view and that will most likely be comprise about 2/3's of the first page. But wait, you say, I have excellent credentials and a great work history . . . surely the recruiter will want to read my entire story!

Just think for a moment . . . if a recruiter has 100 resumes to review on-line for a single opening and takes, on average, 2 minutes to read each resume fully, they have now committed themselves to 200 minutes or 3+ hours to review the resumes for just 1 Monster posting! Do you honestly think that a corporate recruiter who might be carrying 20-30 openings at once has the time to dedicate to a full reading of every resume? No way! And, as an aside, for some postings, a recruiter can receive 300-400 replies! As a result, most recruiters quickly scan the first page of a resume and unless they see something they really like, click the mouse or swipe to move on to the next resume.

So, in this section, our mission is to develop a resume that will be an effective selling tool—one that will quickly "hook" our reader and encourage them to pick our resume from the pack. And, looking to the future, best prepare us *and* our interviewer for the interview itself.

THE METHODOLOGY

The vast majority of resumes go to great lengths to describe what the individual was *responsible* or *accountable* for.   The better resumes may even discuss specific projects that were completed by the candidate. However, what is rarely identified by 95%+ of resumes is the **business benefit** obtained as a result of the candidate's efforts. To personalize this concept . . . based on what is written on your resume, how have you positively changed the companies for which you have worked?   How have you made a difference?   Those resumes that don't sell a candidate's business impact miss the whole point behind what a resume should be.   Additionally, resumes lacking business impact become problematic when candidates attempt to cross industry boundaries. They lack **Transferability of Benefit**. The following example should give you an idea of what I mean by "Transferability of Benefit":

Assume for a moment that we are discussing a candidate, "Harry Winston". Harry is a Manager of Financial Analysis for a manufacturing company. Harry's academic and professional credentials are outstanding.   In the present economy, Harry has had difficulty finding a new position in the manufacturing sector and, as a result, has decided to open his search to include banks, insurance companies, high-tech software firms, etc. He proceeds to send his resume to 100's of these non-manufacturing companies—and gets little or no positive response. Harry is perplexed. He has a great track record, he's "priced right" (dollar-wise) and he knows that he can succeed in any industry—not just manufacturing. However, he gets no "bites". "Why no response?" he asks himself.

In a wide-open economy, where talent is in high-demand and in short supply, companies will often relax their filters—remembering our discussion on compromise earlier—regarding a candidate's *industry* background if all of the other pieces are in place. However, in a tight economy, employers feel that they can become very, very picky. That is, they not only seek candidates with the proper academic credentials and functional experience, but can also demand that candidates have their specific *industry* experience too. This is why our friend Harry is not receiving "bites" on his resume from his non-manufacturing "hit list".

I realize it must seem that companies are being short-sighted to exclude a well-qualified candidate simply because he does not have specific industry experience. However, this is a daily occurrence in the world of recruiting. In a sense, we can't blame the companies for this practice. After all, if the company representative reviewing the resume has no experience in manufacturing, they could very easily make the assumption that Harry's (in our example) experience is not applicable to their non-manufacturing setting. They cannot visualize how Harry's functional experience is easily *transferable* to their industry and company. This is not their fault, though, because Harry has never helped them to understand that the **function** of a Manager of Financial Analysis may be the same in any company or any industry—only the **application** of the function may be somewhat different. As high-impact resume writers, our mission is to *educate* those who read our resumes. Our mission is to help them understand how our experience—even though in a different industry—is portable and can be easily transferred to other industries. This is what I mean by the term *Transferability of Benefit*. So . . . how do we write our resumes so as to achieve this transferability of benefit? Answer: we develop an *action-oriented* resume.

Let's review an example of a "passive" resume and then we'll develop the framework for an *action-oriented* resume. We'll look at examples of each.

AN EXAMPLE OF A "PASSIVE" RESUME

The following is excerpted from an actual resume of a Director of Compensation with a Fortune 100 manufacturing company:

A Major Manufacturing Company   2009 – present
Director of Worldwide Compensation (2000 to present)
Director of Compensation (1998 to 2000)

Directly responsible for the strategic and tactical direction of core pay delivery systems including design and development for 30,000+ salaried and hourly employees. Promoted in 2000 to oversee the management of international compensation and benefits design and administration functions including expatriate administration

- Designed and developed a broad banding philosophy and structure for 7,000 salaried employees and over 300 executives
- Designed and consolidated hourly pay programs and practices for 22,000 hourly employees
- Redesigned sales incentive program for 150 sales representatives and sales management aligned with business strategy
- Redesigned, implemented and administered annual incentive and stock option programs for all employee groups
- Created formal salary structures for employee groups in China and South America
- Team member for corporate-wide shared services project to assess and implement automated compensation processes, manager self-service of administrative functions, and online information for compensation programs
- Co-leader for corporate-wide performance leadership project to implement revised performance appraisal process, merit delivery, competency development, and incentive program to reflect best practice and high-performance culture

Another Large Manufacturing Company   2002 – 2009
Compensation and Benefits Manager

Led the compensation and benefits administration functions. Analyzed sales plan for over 100 sales representatives and presented recommendations for improvement. Developed automated merit delivery tool and presented process recommendations for improvement. Accomplishments included:

- Developed and implemented broad banding structure
- Developed sales incentive and team-based bonus programs
- Project Manager for SAP conversion
- Designed, implemented and monitored all sales incentive and corporate bonus programs
- Developed software program to calculate and process incentive awards for 2,400+ employees worldwide

As you'll note, this is NOT a bad resume. In fact, I would consider it among the better examples of its type. However, while this resume tells the reader what this candidate has done, it reveals very little about how his companies' operating performance have been impacted by all of this "doing". Consequently, unless the resume screener is searching for a specific skill (for example, "SAP" experience—which this candidate has), they may choose to pass on the candidate because they cannot see the impact of his individual effort. Further, if the screener is from outside the manufacturing industry, such as a large investment bank, he or she may feel that projects involving "22,000 hourly employees" may not be applicable to their smaller, primarily white-collar workforce. The screener may interpret this resume in the light of a different "language"—the language of banking—filled with its own jargon and meaning. Net: This screener might just pass on this resume, because ". . . although he looks good, his experience is all manufacturing and it would take him too long to get up-to-speed in our business". They would then click the mouse and move on to the next resume in their pile. One of your primary goals as a high-impact candidate is to prevent the resume screener from *guessing* about your ability to perform in a different industry. Instead, your mission is to educate the screener and demonstrate on paper how your experience can be impactful to companies even outside of your industry background—namely his!

What we'll be doing in this exercise, then, is to develop a *different* type of resume—an *action-oriented* resume that will allow the reader—even those not familiar with your industry or job function—to recognize your impact on a business and be able to mentally "transfer the benefit" of your talent into their industry and company.

WRITING "BULLET POINTS" FOR YOUR RESUME

Our goal then, is to create an "action-oriented" resume. This is a resume that will be filled with projects that you and/or your team have completed—and, highlighting the business benefit obtained from as many of those projects as we can. To help you prepare an action-oriented resume, we're going to use a model, or template. This model will form the basis of a resume that will broaden the industry appeal of your experience by making your contributions evident and your experience *transferable* outside of your particular industry. To build this model, we're going to write your resume in a universal language—a language that is understood by executives everywhere, in every industry—that is, the language of *business impact*.

The first step in the process is for you to carefully review your background and list the projects you have completed or in which you have participated over the course of your career. You will need to list more than just your "responsibilities", but instead, be able to "name" each project or assignment and be able to discuss what you actually delivered or implemented while at each company and in each job. Additionally, I'll want you to be able to identify what the business impact was for each project. This list may be long, but not to worry, I'm going to ask you to choose only the 2-3 most impactful projects on your list from each job to place on your resume. Be advised, this effort could take you as long as 2 hours. You won't get it done in 10 minutes. But, look upon those 2 hours as a necessary means to an end. If you want to generate interviews and become a successful candidate on those interviews, then you have some hard work ahead of you. In the immortal words of somebody, "Nobody said it was going to be easy!"

When you have completed this analysis, we'll be ready for the next step in the process.

Now that you have prepared your list, I would like you to consider the full range of each project—from inception to completion. Your goal will be to write a short, descriptive paragraph describing each project. However, that paragraph should follow the structured methodology or model that we'll discuss next.

The structured model that we will be using to describe your accomplishments will have 5 elements. They are:

1. TYPE OF ACTIVITY
2. Name of project
3. **SCOPE OF PROJECT/TIMELINE**
4. Resources employed
5. BUSINESS BENEFIT OBTAINED

Note the color-coding and different font selection used for each numbered element that we'll be considering for each project. To make it easier to identify each of the 5 elements, the example below will follow this font/color scheme. Although the example we'll use is a Human Resources project, this methodology is equally appropriate for any functional area.

To continue with our model, let's take a "bullet point" from the *passive* resume example shown earlier and expand it using our *action-oriented* model outlined above:

- "Designed and developed a broad banding philosophy and structure for 7,000 salaried employees and over 300 executives."

The expansion should look like this:

DESIGNED AND LED THE CONVERSION OF THE FIRM'S SALARY RANGE STRUCTURE FROM A POINT–FACTOR (HAY) SYSTEM TO A "BROADBAND" SYSTEM. The roadband project affected over 7,000 professional employees, includin 300 executives, coverin 25 discrete salary ran es. **SUCCESSFUL IMPLEMENTATION REQUIRED AN ANALYSIS OF ALL AFFECTED JOBS FOR CONTENT AND IMPACT ON THE FIRM'S OPERATING RESULTS, ALONG WITH DEVELOPING**

CAREER "TRACKS" TO SUPPORT THE NEW, BANDED RANGES. Utilized internal staff and external resources over this 3-month project. AS A RESULT OF THE NEW STRUCTURE'S IMPLEMENTATION, 25 SALARY RANGES WERE DECREASED TO 8 BANDS RESULTING IN A 12% INCREASE IN EMPLOYEE SATISFACTION AS MEASURED BY OUR FIRM'S ORGANIZATIONAL HEALTH SURVEY. BOTH RECRUITING AND RETENTION HAVE BEEN ENHANCED AS A RESULT OF THE NEW SALARY/PAY STRUCTURE.

Note that this "bullet-point" description of the "Broadbanding" project contained all five elements of our model.

For your resume, you'll need 2-3 *bullets* just like the above for each company for which you have worked and for each job you have held—we're only going to use 2 for each job so you'll need to pick the most marketable to build a resume that will really sell your experience. Developing a resume using this model will separate you from the candidate who just describes the jobs they've had ("responsible for" or "accountable for")—versus how they influenced and impacted the business. The former type of resume may mean nothing to the reader if they are in a different industry, country, etc. What we want our readers to see is that your ability to contribute will not be diminished by a change in industry. To do this, you will have to describe your "deliverables" to the reader in such a manner that eliminates guesswork and assumption. I believe in telling a company exactly what you've done and how you have positively impacted the business. Writing a high-impact resume is not the time to be modest!

You can also use a Bullet Point/Deliverables Matrix such as shown on the next page to develop your "bullets". For some, a Matrix may be an easier means of visually itemizing deliverables and impact. However, either method will work.

My guess is that after you've completed this analysis of your background, your concern might be, "Sounds great, but if I write a paragraph for each of my projects, my resume will be 10 pages long!" And, this would be correct if we included all of the information generated for each "bullet point". We will not. Instead, you'll need to synthesize each descriptive paragraph and utilize only the name/function of the project and the "results" or business impact derived. However, your extra efforts will not be wasted. Please retain your initial descriptions and set them aside—they'll come in handy later when we discuss "The 5 Questions".

On the next page is an example of a Bullet Point/Deliverables Matrix

Bullet Point/Deliverables Matrix

Company/Role	Project/Responsibility	Actual Deliverable/s	Business Impact
Major Manufacturing Company/ Director of Worldwide Compensation	Hay (point-factor) to Broadband conversion affecting 7,000 professional employees. Led a team of 3 on the project over a 3-month period	Analyzed all salary ranges and jobs. Decreased 25 salary ranges to only 8 job bands.	Employee satisfaction increased by 12%. Recruiting effectiveness and retention increased.
Major Manufacturing Company/ Director of Compensation	Houston/Toronto office consolidation. Led effort to identify cost savings and analyze office/staff expenses required to carry 2 offices.	Reduced headcount by 30 FTEs, subleased Toronto facility and developed relocation/severance packages for transferred/terminated staff.	Lowered admin expenses by $250,000 and increased efficiency by 8%.
And so on . . .			

Using either method (5 Point Model or Matrix should help you produce a resume that looks something like this:

EXAMPLE OF ACTION-ORIENTED RESUME

2009 to Present	<u>Large Energy Company</u> Vice President, Compensation & Benefits

Reporting to the Senior Vice President of Human Resources for design, development and administration of executive, base, and incentive compensation programs and benefit plans for 12,000 employees in U.S. & Canada.

- Designed a Board-directed Executive Compensation Program for the top 65 executives in company. Result: Introduced market competitive plan covering base, bonus and long-term incentives which eliminated turnover to competition.

- Implemented consolidated benefit program for all business units. Result: Limited medical plan increases to one-half of national average without increasing employee deductibles or co-insurance costs.

- Consolidated U.S. and Canadian Human Resources function into the Houston, Texas office. Result: Improved administrative efficiency and lowered expenses by over $250,000.

- Designed new Canadian benefits program and sourced to three vendors. Result: Reduced annual plan costs by over C$500,000 while improving employee coverage.

- Directed the outsourcing of 215 unemployment insurance state tax filings and administration to one vendor. Result: Lowered costs by more than $500,000 annually.

2002 to 2009	<u>Major Consulting Firm</u> Director, Global Compensation

Reporting to the Vice President-Human Resources and the Compensation Committee for developing and maintaining compensation programs for consultants worldwide and administrative staff.

- Established a global compensation system. Result: Achieved consistent application of compensation across 35 countries.

- Designed executive compensation program for the top 100 performing officers. Result: Gained Board approval for stock option plan still in use today.

- Developed and administered stock option award program for "newly elected officers." Result: Attracted highly-rated talent from other recognized strategic consulting firms.

Note the difference in the two examples. The action-oriented resume leaves nothing to the reader's imagination. It is evident upon reading it that this candidate has not only been "responsible for" or completed projects, but has also had a demonstrable impact on the business. Ask yourself this question: of the two resumes, which version is more likely to generate an interview?

If you're wondering how much time it will take to complete this exercise, then wonder no more . . . to do the job correctly, it should take you 2-3 hours to complete this type of analysis and synthesis. However, as we progress, you'll quickly connect the time you've invested with the many benefits you'll receive through the completion of this exercise. Building an "action-oriented" resume is well worth the effort and will allow you to kill many birds with the same stone. Specifically:

1. You will create an action/results-oriented selling document (your resume) with "pick me" qualities.
2. By default, you'll get to know your resume very well. You'll re-familiarize yourself with your own background—this is essential if you want to deliver high-impact answers to your

interviewer's questions (as we'll discuss in "The 5 Questions).

3. During the interview, you will be able to guide your interviewer in a direction that focuses on your strengths.

This last point is very important. If you have already been interviewing, you know that most interviewers base their initial set of questions on the data you've provided in your resume. This being true, why not develop a resume that directs your interviewer's initial questions to highlight your proven accomplishments and deliverables? This will help to get your interview off to a fast start!

Again, I'm not implying that building this type of resume will be quick or easy—it won't be either. However, if you are serious about securing a new position and you want to increase the likelihood of having your resume selected from the huge pool of available candidates, and be in the best position to be viewed as an outstanding candidate during the interview, then building an action-oriented resume is one of the critical tasks that you'll need to complete.

"CAREER SUMMARIES" AND CLAIM STATEMENTS (I.E. HYPERBOLE VS. REALITY)

As a footnote to the development of your new resume, let's deal with one of my pet biases— the ever-popular "Career Summary" section that usually begins the resume. Typically, I find this section filled with "claim statements". As an example, here's one of the milder examples of a "Career Summary" section from an actual resume that I received just yesterday:

> "Dynamic executive with a strategic, metric driven, results-oriented, innovative and problem-solving approach. Possesses the ability to influence all members of the organization as a strategic business partner and positively impact the bottom line."

Need I go on? I think you get the message. This individual has filled the opening section of their resume with totally self-serving and self-aggrandizing statements — without any foundation upon which to base them. In other words, this person has filled the air with hyperbole (according to Webster, ". . . an intentional exaggeration not intended to be taken literally") – except in this case, I think the candidate really means to be taken literally. Unfortunately, without a single statement of fact to support them, these adjectives and descriptors (dynamic, strategic, innovative, etc.) are perceived by the reader as empty and lacking substance. From the opening seconds of scanning this resume, the reader is already mentally thinking, "Yeah, sure. Yada, Yada, Yada." As a result, he may not continue his scan with the level of scrutiny required to make certain the resume winds up in the "Yes" pile. This is why I stress so strongly that we should always have fact and data to support all of our statements—both those in writing and those we speak. We want to be perceived as believable and credible. This is to our advantage.

Skipping the hyperbole, here's a much stronger "Career Summary":

> "Metric-driven Human Resources executive with proven success in the delivery of business-changing strategies in the areas of talent management, executive compensation, organizational development, organizational effectiveness and union relations."

In this Career Summary, you'll note that the focus is on the functional expertise of the candidate, not on all of his sterling personal qualities. Once you've adopted the High-Impact Resume methodology, your resume will be able to immediately support the above statements as your reader reviews your "bullet points" describing your experiences in Talent Management, Executive Compensation, Organizational Development, etc.

Because it is such an important concept to understand, we're going to revisit this whole issue of "Claim Statements" and "Fact Statements" later in this book. However, if you'd like, you can skip ahead to that discussion. Reading it will give you an idea of how important it is to support every statement we make—both on the resume and during the interview itself—if our goal is to be viewed as believable and memorable.

So, again, be careful how you begin your resume with the "Career Summary" section. Being perceived as credible—in all that we say and do—is the perception we want to maintain throughout the entire recruiting process.

WRITING HIGH-IMPACT COVER LETTTERS

Now that you've developed a high-impact resume, it's now time to discuss your cover letter. Having read tens of thousands of cover letters, I can state categorically that most do not serve the candidate well. However, when I do read an excellent cover letter, it encourages me to read the resume and get serious about the candidate. We've already discussed the time parameters most recruiters set on scanning each resume—it's a time-bounded business and you have only a few seconds to "hook" your reader. So how do we go about developing a cover letter that generates the interest of your reader?

First, let me say, that I am a minimalist regarding cover letters. My approach is to make your point quickly, back it up with results and deliverables and then get out of the way. Too often I read cover letters that attempt to outdo the resume. These cover letters are too long, contain unnecessary and often irrelevant information, and directed to a general audience. They rarely target the search I am conducting. While it may be efficient to send your resume along with a "vanilla" cover letter, doing so will most likely cause you too undershoot or overshoot your target — that is, the specific position for which you are applying. I recognize that it takes extra time and effort to "personalize" your cover letter, but if you're interested in generating interviews and being perceived as a high-impact candidate, then it's worth the investment in research and time.

So how do you write this type of cover letter—one that generates phone calls and interviews? Let's get specific:

1. Take the time to do your homework and find out the correct name (including spelling) and title of the person to whom you are writing your cover letter. Many ads or postings have the name of the recruiter or company contact in them. For those that don't, why not call the company directly and find out who is recruiting for the position for which you're applying? Or, you can go to a site such as LinkedIn and find out who might be the possible hiring authority. If these efforts do not generate a name— and often companies place "blind ads" (those that don't identify the company or recruiter), then this is not an option. But for those ads that do identify the firm and contact, use the information.

2. Develop an action-oriented first sentence geared specifically to the position for which you're applying. To do this, we're going to resurrect your resume. For this example, we're going to use the resume already shown as our model. You're applying for a

Director of Compensation role. Your first line should read, "I am a proven leader with 20 years of experience leading high-performing compensation and benefit organizations. I feel I can make a contribution to the growth of your business as your Director of Compensation." Again, we're hypothesizing that the firm has advertised for a Director of Compensation. Remember our earlier discussion on "Claim Statements"? Needless to say, your next section had better support your claim statement of being a "proven leader of high-performing compensation organizations". You've already done the hard work on your resume, so let's use the "bullets" you've already prepared to convert our claims to fact statements in the next paragraph.

3. In the next paragraph, utilize 1-2 (but no more than 2) of the "bullets" you've already prepared for your resume. From the posting or ad, identify the experiences that the company seems to be seeking and place those in this section. For our example, we've read that the company is interested in candidates with Board level experience, executive compensation experience and international experience. Here are "bullets" you could use:

- Designed and implemented a Board-directed Executive Compensation Program for the top 65 executives in company. Result: Introduced a market competitive plan covering base, bonus and long-term incentives which eliminated turnover to competition.

- Established a global compensation system. Result: Achieved consistent application of compensation across 35 countries.

4. In your third and final paragraph, make every attempt to target your prospective employer with your experience and your knowledge of the company. For example, if the company is identified, perform a Google (or similar) search and find current information about the firm (for example, from press releases). Let's say your search has uncovered that the company has made an acquisition of a foreign company. You can then very easily place a sentence in the third paragraph such as this:

> Investigating your company, I noticed that the firm has just acquired Hyperion, Inc. a British firm. I feel my experience in international compensation and benefits could be an asset as you integrate that company into your organization.

The benefit of doing this is that 99% of candidates won't make the effort. Demonstrating that you "know" the company and the latest events affecting it will separate you from the other 100+ cover letters/resumes the screener is reading. In short, just from reading your cover letter, the screener starts forming perceptions about you as someone who does their homework and is a serious candidate for the role.

5. When the ad or posting requests salary information, you have a choice to make. You can either comply with the company's request or not. My counsel is to **not** include the information—even if it is "required". If you are a well-qualified candidate with an on-target, high-impact resume, do you really think that the company is not going to call you if you don't include the salary information they are seeking? Remember, great candidates are very hard to find—a company is just not going to pass on you as a candidate because you didn't place your salary information on your cover letter. If you're on target with their specification, at a minimum you are going to receive a call from the company—if for no other reason than to find out what you are earning and if you are in the salary range for the position. My preference is to always hold on salary data until it is necessary—as in when you're asked for the information during the interview (more about this later). Our goal is to get the

company representative to call us so that we have a chance to sell our background and experiences. Prematurely divulging salary information can stop the call before it is made.

Here's our cover letter—short and targeted to our hypothetical posting:

Dear Ms. Habersham:

I am a proven leader with 20 years of experience leading high performing compensation and benefit organizations. I think I can make a contribution to the growth of your business as your **Director of Compensation**. A few of my accomplishments include:

- Designed and implemented a Board-directed Executive Compensation Program for the top 65 executives in company. **Result**: Introduced a market competitive plan covering base, bonus and long-term incentives which eliminated turnover to competition.

- Established a global compensation system. **Result**: Achieved consistent application of compensation across 35 countries.

Investigating your company, I noticed that the firm has just acquired Hyperion, Inc. a British firm. I feel my experience in international compensation and benefits could be an asset as you integrate that company into your organization.

Thank you for considering my application. I am available for an interview or a telephone conversation at your convenience.

Sincerely,

Again, our cover letter is short and targeted to both the position and the company.

Make certain you've checked and double-checked both your resume and cover letter for errors, both grammatical and spelling. Nothing is a quicker turnoff for most recruiters than resumes or cover letters with misspelled words, poor grammar or sloppy presentation. Don't rely on a spell checker exclusively. Spell checkers will catch most misspelled words, but not all. However, they will *not* identify incorrect word usage such as "sea" when you wanted to write "see" (homonyms). They will often miss poorly constructed sentences—which can occur when you've "copy/pasted" a word or words into a sentence. Lastly, save your resume screener eye strain. Most likely, your resume will be viewed on a smaller screen computer monitor, laptop or tablet, so you'll want to use a standard font (Arial works well, with Calibri being my current favorite) and a reasonable size (12 point). Remember, at this point, the only image the company has of you is what they have seen from your cover letter and resume. Make certain that your resume and cover letter represent you well by creating the image you seek to project.

Now that you've gotten to know your resume better (and your business impact) and have the formula for developing high-impact cover letters, you now need to dedicate time getting to know *yourself* better. This is the purpose of our next section. What follows in this next section is a series of simple, yet powerful exercises designed to get you thinking about your career—specifically, what you will need to do to achieve success and where you can best achieve it. The output of all of this contemplation and analysis will be a *Success Matrix*—a document that will define the type of company, culture and environment, and role that will have the greatest likelihood of facilitating your success.

GETTING TO KNOW YOURSELF

Have you ever thought about what you really want from your next position and company? Just think a second. Sure, you want more "challenge and opportunity" and compensation, but have you ever thought about . . .

- Do you want long-term career growth within one company or within your industry/profession? In other words, are you interested in working for one firm the majority of your career, or do you seek a company where you can gain marketable experience that will prepare you for your next job in the next company?

- What would you like to learn that is <u>new</u>, in your next role? And, in what areas would you like to further enhance your current skill set?

- How will your next job prepare you for the next job after that—either within your new company or in firms that you may join in the future?

- Do you seek personal recognition or are you satisfied with working on challenging and complex projects without much feedback from your peers or bosses?

- Where you would like to be career-wise and personally in 5 years? 10 years? 20 years?

- What types of people do you most enjoy working with?

- How important is salary? What is the salary offer that you would accept?

- What types of environments and assignments have made you successful in the past? Will this new position offer opportunities and an environment and culture that are similar?

- Why have you failed in the past? Let's be honest, all of us have failed at one time or the other. Would the new company or job replicate those conditions?

- And so on . . .

Most candidates enter the interviewing process without having spent more than 15 seconds truly thinking through these issues. Sure, they have thought about how much more money they would *like* to make, and which job title would be most attractive. They may have even thought about the responsibilities of the new job and whether they would enjoy them. However, the vast majority of candidates have not considered their potential new job in the context of the environment and culture of the company they'd be joining; or like a chess master looking several moves ahead, how that job will prepare them for the next job and the next job after that one. Is it any wonder then, that job changes are so frequent? It is amazing to think that an individual can make 2-3 moves in quick succession and walk away at the end of that 4-6 year period with so little to show for that huge investment in "career time". Unfortunately, it happens with regularity! Again, my goal for you is that you will *do your homework* <u>*before*</u> *you take the test*. The investment of time on the front-end will pay huge benefits over the course of your career.

THE IMPORTANCE OF UNDERSTANDING COMPANY CULTURE

The single most important data point you can gain prior to and during your interview is an understanding of your target firm's corporate culture. Without understanding corporate culture, a good employment decision is just a matter of luck, not design. Bear in mind, that despite their outward similarities, all companies possess a different, or discrete, *corporate culture*. So, just what is this thing called *corporate culture*?

Corporate culture is defined as the "shared values" that contribute to the successful performance of the company and the individuals working there. What this means from an interviewing standpoint, is that a great candidate for Company A, may not be a suitable candidate for an identical position at Company B. We have to get over the thought that just because we have been successful at our company, that we can go anywhere, to any company, and work for any boss, and achieve the same or greater level of success. Read *The Wall Street Journal* and start counting how many executives leave successful careers at one company, move to another firm, and promptly fall on their face. These executives didn't just get stupid all of a sudden or lose their ability. They are smart people—having already "made their bones" through multiple successes in their prior firms. However, whenever you read of a quick entrance and exit, most likely that executive failed to appreciate the critical nature of a firm's corporate culture. They never stopped to consider that their past success had been a function of not only their own skill, but also being in the right corporate "culture"—one that could best utilize their skills and talents most effectively. Even Michael Jordan, the greatest basketball player of all time (my opinion) achieved true <u>mediocrity</u> when he left the Chicago Bulls in 1993 (after leading his team to 3 consecutive NBA championships), and began a career in major league baseball with the AA Birmingham Barons—a Chicago White Sox farm team. After a year of hitting barely .200, Michael returned to the NBA, and the environment and culture for which he was best suited, and led the Bulls to 3 more championships! So, what's the lesson here?

Before making a move, consider your career. What has made you successful? What are the qualities and attributes present in your current company that have contributed to your success? If you have failed or not performed to your expectations in the past, what was there about that company's environment or culture that may have contributed to that failure? Needless to say, when you can answer these questions you'll be on your way to begin best targeting those companies where you'll have the greatest likelihood of achieving success. Knowing a firm's culture and your suitability within it <u>will</u> help you to make better career decisions.

You might ask, "This is all very interesting, but how do I find out about the firm's culture? Where can I get this type of information?" These are good questions. Throughout this section, I'll provide you with a methodology that will help you answer these questions. I'll also give you several questions that you can ask that will help you ferret out the nature of the corporate culture in a prospective employer and an exercise to complete that will help you gain a better understanding of the type of culture that is most likely to facilitate your success. There are even websites available that are useful in getting the goods on what working in your target company is really like. First, though, let's gain a bit of self-awareness and understanding.

THE VALUE SYSTEM ANALYSIS

As the first step in gaining the self-awareness that will be critical to your pre-interview preparation, I'd like you to complete a simple and quick exercise I call a "Value System Analysis". Completing a Value System Analysis will help you to focus on the factors that influenced you to join your current company and the factors that have caused you to stay. This exercise will be our first insight into the organizational values that must be present to provide you with the greatest likelihood of achieving short and long-term career success. Understanding these values will help you get to the core of what there is about a firm's culture that creates an environment geared for *your* success. Coincidentally, this same exercise will prepare you to better answer your interviewer's questions when you're on the firing line. In the next four exercises you are going to be required to consider issues that will form the basis of the questions that you are sure to be asked on your next interview.

Your goal, as you complete the next 4 exercises, is to clearly define the best type of culture, environment and company for which you would like to work. This type of company will offer you the highest probability of achieving success—both short and long-term. Let's begin the analysis. Read the questions on the form below, consider your answers, and then fill out the form.

CORPORATE VALUE SYSTEM ANALYSIS

(Considering your current organization or your most resent company)

1. What was the single, most important factor behind you joining your current company?

2. What would make it hardest to leave your company?

3. Considering the jobs that you have had, what did you enjoy most about them?

4. How highly does/did your company value its people? If your firm does not value its employees highly, to what degree does this bother you?

5. What should a company "stand for" (or . . . The company I want to work for will have these values)?

As an aside, I offer this same exercise to participants in my corporate training sessions and in my graduate classes where 90%+ of my students are working full-time. In the past 20 years, over 3,000 individuals have responded to these same questions. Care to see what the consensus has been and match them against your answers?

RESULTS OF: CORPORATE VALUE SYSTEM ANALYSIS

(1450 respondents–responses listed in order of frequency)

THINKING ABOUT YOUR CURRENT ORGANIZATION

(OR YOUR MOST RECENT COMPANY):

1. What was the single, most important factor behind you joining your current company?
   - Corporate culture compatible to own values
   - Compensation/Benefits
   - Career growth potential of initial job

2. What would make it hardest to leave your company?
   - Personal relationships with co-workers
   - Challenging current job responsibilities
   - Corporate culture
   - Fear of the "unknown"
   - Inertia (easier to stay than to leave)

3. Considering the jobs that you have had, what did you enjoy most about them?
   - People
   - Challenge of job
   - Autonomy/"power" of position

4. How highly does/did your company value its people? If your firm does not value its employees highly, does this bother you?
   - "Not Valued" over "Valued" by a 2.5:1 margin

5. What should a company "stand for" (or, the company I want to work for will have these values)?
   - Employee-oriented environment
   - Focus on mutual benefit (Company does well, people do well)
   - Industry leader
   - Integrity/honesty

I'm going to bet that your answers to the questions above were similar to previous respondents. As human beings, we all share a very similar "wish list" when defining the attributes that represent desirable corporate qualities. The next time you start thinking that what you want in a company is so different from what everyone else is seeking, consider the Corporate Value System Analysis. Again, you'll find that most people think similarly about the type of firms with which they want to be associated. The values identified in this survey define the culture of winning organizations. If you analyze *Fortune* magazine's, "100 Best Companies to Work For" report (appearing typically in the first February issue), you find that these values are shared by virtually all of the listed Top 100 companies. The companies appearing on this list are not only considered great places to work—with outstanding corporate cultures—but are also among the leaders in operating performance (sales growth, profitability, market share, etc.) in their respective industries. The companies on the "100 Best" list are all winners. Needless to say, most of us would be excited to interview with, and be hired by, any of the companies on this list—because everybody wants to play on the winning team!

To get us even closer to preparing our final working document, the "Success Matrix" (a set of criteria that defines the culture, environment and "competencies" that will make our success possible in a new organization), I'd like you next to complete a "Pre-Interview Questionnaire".

THE PRE-INTERVIEW QUESTIONNAIRE

Again, you're going to have to invest time thinking through what is important to you in your current company, and by extrapolation, your next company. To wit:

PLAYING 20 QUESTIONS: ASKING QUESTIONS TO DETERMINE CORPORATE CULTURE

(USE YOUR CURRENT OR PREVIOUS COMPANY AS YOUR REFERENCE POINT)

1. What makes people successful at XYZ Company?
2. Why do people fail?
3. What do you most enjoy (and what gets you most frustrated) about working at XYZ?
4. What is the principal cause of employee turnover? Do you feel that reason is justified?
5. How important are "politics" within the firm?
6. How will my performance be measured?
7. How frequently will I receive my performance appraisal?

8. What do you feel that I will need to accomplish within my first year to be considered successful?

9. Why is this position available?

10. While doing my research, I noticed that (pick a current event from a press release of Google search, such as: the opening of a new plant, IPO, new product line launch, change in accounting methodology, etc.) . . . How do you think this will affect the business as a whole? What impact will this have on the department/role?

11. Were any candidates available internally for this role? Did anyone express interest in this role?

12. How often does XYZ promote from within?

13. How would you describe the culture/environment within XYZ?

14. Do you encourage employees to meet with each other socially at XYZ?

15. How would you describe my potential boss as a person?

16. Assuming that I deliver excellent performance, how long would you anticipate that I would remain in this job? What do you feel my next step/job will be?

17. Will I have an opportunity to meet my potential peers during this interview process?
18. How does XYZ communicate changes in corporate policy?
19. How much contact will I have with senior management?
20. How would you describe me as a candidate for this role, compared to others with whom you've spoken?

And so on . . .

After you've answered these questions about your current company/job, keep these questions and your answers handy because we'll be using them later. As part of our pre-interview preparation, I'm going to ask you to answer these same questions with your *next* company in mind—that is, the company with which you will be interviewing. Any questions that you can't answer before the interview, will make for great questions to ask your interviewers at the point where they ask you, "Do you have any questions?" They're a bit more powerful and thoughtful than asking, "Can you tell me about your benefit plan?" Coming prepared to ask these questions on an interview is going to set you apart from the vast majority of candidates. Your interviewers are going to look at you with wonderment and awe, as in . . . "Wow, good questions! This candidate has actually thought about this interview!" Asking good questions is also a great means of answering that all-important question: what is it really like to work at this company? Or, put more simply: "Can I succeed in this company?"

PLANNING FOR THE LONG-TERM

WHAT POSITION AM I WORKING TOWARDS? – INDIVIDUAL EXERCISE

Here's another area to consider . . . what are your long-term goals? Will the role for which you'll be interviewing better prepare you for the next job and the next job after that? Will it provide you with new skills that will enable you to weather an economic downturn? Will it increase your marketability during boom times?

When planning for the long-term it is very important to consider that all of us will have an *end job* – that is, the final job we will hold when we reach retirement age. Of course, that age will vary depending on the individual. When considering what that end job might be, we need to analyze our current position and the path that we have been taking. The quick thought exercise that follows will help you analyze your current role and what you'll need to do career-wise to achieve your end objective. Bear in mind, this end objective does not have to be chiseled in stone—it may (and probably will) change many times over the first 20 years of your "career time". However, it's never too early to start thinking about where you'd ultimately like to be in your career.

PLANNING FOR THE LONG TERM

What is my "End Job" and What Must I Do to Get There

1. What position/level are you working towards in your career?

2. Considering the current state of your career, what additional experience, exposure, training, development, etc. do feel will be necessary for you to achieve your "End Job"?

3. Is it possible for you to reach your "End Job" from within your current company?
   - If possible: Are you willing to prepare and wait for that opportunity to develop within your current firm? Or, would the waiting ultimately cause you to seek that role outside of your company?

   - If not possible: Why not?

THE SUCCESS MATRIX

Most candidates enter into the interview process without having considered the questions or having completed the exercises in this section. Sure, they've thought about "the job", but not in the context of the larger whole—that is, the corporate culture in which they'll be working and whether that corporate culture fits their individual style. Is it any wonder that job changes are so frequent?

Now that you've had an opportunity to do some thinking about your career, goals and objectives, it's time to integrate this disparate group of thoughts into a single document. The output of this integration is our next exercise. Our goal is to create a single document that defines the parameters necessary for us to achieve career success. I call this document a "Success Matrix". It is a very simple document that holds great power. If you've done your homework properly, a completed Success Matrix will clearly define the culture and environment that is most likely to facilitate your success. The Success Matrix will define your strengths so that when you interview for a new position you will be able to emphasize those strengths! It will also identify your developmental needs, so that you can focus on only those companies that offer the skills and experiences you need for targeted career growth. This is in stark contrast to most scenarios, where companies hire candidates who have the skills and experience that they (the company) need—while not caring whether they can provide the developmental opportunities that will help the candidate reach his or her long-term goals! From personal experience you can probably relate very well to jobs that you've held in the past where the scales were decided tipped in the favor of the employer—when it came time to measuring the balance of what you've invested vs. what you have received. We want to make certain that we are going to receive as much from the employment relationship as we are investing—that is, our goal is to achieve a balance between what we will get (compensation, career growth, new skills, etc.) from our new company vs. what we will give or invest (our lives, personal time, career time, physical and mental effort, opportunity cost, etc.).

Imagine being able to interview with only those companies who you already know possess the attributes that will increase the likelihood of your success. What a great deal! Not only will you waste less time in the short-term interviewing with non-conforming companies, but more important, over the long-term you will waste less *career-time* working at companies or on jobs that will never help you achieve your long-term goals. Armed with this insight, you will gain another important benefit—you will approach the interview process in a decidedly more focused manner.

MY SUCCESS MATRIX	
MY IDEAL COMPANY WILL HAVE THESE ATTRIBUTES (ITS CULTURE):	A COMPANY WOULD WANT TO HIRE ME BECAUSE I HAVE:
	MY LONG TERM CAREER GOALS ARE:
	TO MEET MY LONG-TERM CAREER GOALS I MUST GAIN THESE SKILLS/EXPERIENCES:

To get you started, I've provided a sample of a completed "Success Matrix", using a Human Resources professional as a model:

MY SUCCESS MATRIX

(SAMPLE: FOR A HUMAN RESOURCES PROFESSIONAL)

MY IDEAL COMPANY WILL HAVE THESE ATTRIBUTES (CORPORATE STRATEGY/ CORPORATE CULTURE):	A COMPANY WOULD WANT TO HIRE ME BECAUSE I HAVE: (FOR EACH "BULLET" YOU'LL NEED TO A SPECIFIC ACCOMPLISHMENT OR DELIVERABLE TO TRANSFORM YOUR CLAIM STATEMENT INTO A FACT STATEMENT)
CORPORATE STRATEGY	⊕ CREATIVITY AND PROVEN ABILITY TO INNOVATE
	⊕ WILLINGNESS TO TAKE RISKS
⊕ CUSTOMER FOCUSED	⊕ INTEGRITY
⊕ BEING #1	⊕ DESIRE TO ACHIEVE EXCELLENCE
⊕ GLOBAL FOCUS	⊕ FUNCTIONAL DEPTH AND EXPERTISE (E.G LISTING OF HR
⊕ CREATES MARKETS VS. "ME TOO"	SPECIFIC TECHNICAL OR FUNCTIONAL SKILLS)
	⊕ EXCELLENT ORAL AND WRITTEN COMMUNICATION SKILLS
CORPORATE CULTURE	⊕ ABILITY TO WORK EFFECTIVELY ON A TEAM
	MY LONG-TERM CAREER GOALS ARE:
⊕ CREATIVITY	
⊕ PLAY HARD, WORK HARDER	⊕ FUNCTION HEAD (E.G. SVP HR) OF FORTUNE 500 CORP.
⊕ TEAM ORIENTATION	⊕ OBTAIN MBA FROM FIRST-TIER UNIVERSITY
⊕ PEOPLE OF THE FIRM'S #1 INVEST-MENT	⊕ ALTERNATIVELY, LEAD LARGE, MULIT-DISCIPLINE STAFF WITH P&L RESPONSIBILITY IN A "LINE MANAGEMENT" ROLE.
⊕ CONTINUOUS LEARNING	⊕ BUILD EQUITY POSITION WITHIN A FIRM
⊕ RESULTS ORIENTATION	**TO MEET MY LONG-TERM GOALS I MUST GAIN THESE SKILLS/ EXPERIENCES:**
⊕ HIRING THE BEST	⊕ APPLY FOR ADMISSION TO NORTHWESTERN UNIVERSITY/ KELLOGG
	⊕ MANAGE LARGE COMPENSATION PROJECT WITH 4-5 TEAM MEMBERS IN NEXT ROLE, AND PROGRESSIVELY INCREASE NUMBER/SCOPE OF PROJECTS AND STAFF SIZE
	⊕ CONTINUE TO DEVELOP LEADERSHIP SKILLS THROUGH CORPORATE TRAINING PROGRAMS
	⊕ INCREASE VISIBILITY IN FIRM BY VOLUNTEERING TO LEAD CORPORATE RESTRUCTURING INITIATIVE
	⊕ GAIN GREATER EXPERIENCE IN ORGANIZATIONAL DEVELOPMENT AND SUCCESSION PLANNING
	⊕ INCREASE NEGOTIATION SKILLS THROUGH ATTENDING WORKSHOP
	⊕ ENHANCE GROUP PRESENTATION SKILLS BY ATTENDING *THE EXECUTIVE TECHNIQUE* TRAINING PROGRAM

A well-done Success Matrix defines the criteria for your success—both short and long term. You will be able to identify: 1.) The type of company, as defined by its strategy and culture, that is most likely to facilitate your success; 2.) What you are "selling"— that is, your strengths or significant accomplishments that you will want to emphasize on your interview; 3.) Your long-term career goals or "end job"; and, 4.) The areas of growth or specialized skills you will need to develop to attain your "end job". We will revisit each of these 4 areas and discuss their implementation in Section IV, The Interview ("The 5 Questions"). Taking a quick jump ahead, we are going to use the Success Matrix to help us formulate the basis of the answers we'll be giving to our interviewers; and, we will use it as a "compass" to effectively guide the interview to a favorable outcome.

THE "BOSS SIDE OF THE EQUATION"

Beyond culture and environment, the next most important relationship to understand and one that should be among your key decision points when considering a role in a new firm is the *Boss Side of the Equation*. Why so, you ask?

Bosses are key contributors and facilitators to our success. Think for a moment how much influence a good boss (a bad one for that matter) has had on your career. A boss is in a singular position to truly influence our destinies. They determine the assignments we get. They determine how much "credit" we get for a project well done. They influence our salary increases and our ability to get promoted; and to a large extent can influence what others think about us—particular those more senior to us. After all, who do you think is the primary input and conduit for information about you passed to senior management? A great boss can have a profound effect on your future growth. A poor boss can destroy or significantly lessen your chances for promotion. As a result, the "boss side of the equation" or relationship is one to be truly considered when moving through the interview process. Unfortunately, most candidates focus on the job responsibilities, company, peer group, etc., but cast a totally blind eye to the person who will be their boss. Many candidates think that they're just so good that even if they don't like their boss on the interview, that it won't be problem. They feel that they'll be promoted so quickly that soon that person will be working for them and then, they ". . . can really straighten him out!" So, there's no need to focus on the "boss side of the equation" . . . right?

A good boss (that is, someone we can work for effectively) can be ferreted out during the interview. He or she should be willing to listen to your ideas. They will express a sincere interest in you, not only as a candidate, but as a person, too! You will feel a connection or chemistry with a good boss—even on a first interview. I always ask my candidates if they liked their potential boss based on their interview experience. As an aside, by the word "liked", I don't mean that you are seeking to become new BFFs with the individual; but instead, do you believe personally in what your potential new boss "stands for"? Is their value system in concert with yours? Do you feel a "connection" with the individual?

A few of the attributes I ask my candidates to assess in their potential boss are:

1. **Good Listening Skills** – Does the boss listen to your ideas on the interview? Do they seem genuinely interested in your values as well as your accomplishments and technical skills?

2. **Sincere Engagement** – During the interview, did your boss give you their undivided attention, or did

he make you feel as if you were a distraction from the main event in his overly-full workday?

3. **Ability to Respond to Your Questions** – When you asked questions, did you get a straight and honest answer? Were you able to ask tough questions without generating defensive behavior? As an example, I always like to have my candidates ask potential bosses for their assessment of the department's or team's performance. For me personally, a boss who is not willing to respond openly, or treats questions as an invasion of their privacy, or answers with a number of excuses as to why this or that didn't happen, or places blame on members of his team directly, is a boss who I'd be very reticent (as in, no way) to join. Red flags would be popping up all over the field! Just remember, a boss who does not take personal responsibility for their department's performance is one that could very likely be naming you as the reason he failed a year from now, while interviewing a future candidate.

4. **Are they Respected by Their Peers** – Observe the behavior of your boss' peers while they

interact with him or her during the interview process. Is there a mutual respect? Does your boss appear relaxed and confident when interacting with his peers or his own boss? This is a key area to observe, as a boss who does not command the respect of his peers or superiors is probably not going to be able to help you from a career point-of-view. A boss who is considered weak by his peers or superiors will not be in a position to push for you at promotion or salary increase time. They will not be able to provide you with the "covering fire" that you'll need if you get into a dispute or conflict with another department or individual. They may be unable or unwilling to go to bat for you when you need a little extra "push" to obtain scarce resources necessary to get your job done. If you don't feel confident in your boss's ability to be a leader or to maintain the respect of his peers/superiors, then you'd better hoist a big red flag in your mind while considering the role.

In short, consider this truism: interview relationships with the boss are not like fine wine—they do not improve with age. If anything, they degrade once you become an employee. This means that if you *assume* that a questionable choice for a boss is going to improve with the passage of time or after they get the chance to have you on their team, you are very likely on a collision course with disaster!

Make the boss side of the equation a critical element in your overall decision on any job/company.

JUST HOW WELL DO YOU KNOW THIS COMPANY?

As important as knowing your resume and knowing yourself is for interview success, so is knowing a whole lot about the company that will be interviewing you.

One of the all-time embarrassing moments in my own interview life came in 1979. At that time, I was an HR Manager with American Hospital Supply Corporation (now, Cardinal Health, Inc.) in Chicago. I had been contacted by a recruiter to interview for a division Director, Human Resources role with A.O. Smith Corporation in Milwaukee, Wisconsin. Well, given the fact that I had been recruiting for 5 years at that point, I felt that I knew a little about every company and quite a bit about most—after all, wasn't it my job to know who the competition was? As a result, I did absolutely no homework on A.O. Smith prior to the interview—confident that what little I did know would be enough to "bull" my way through the interview.

My interview was set for 5:30 PM on a Thursday. I arrived in the lobby on time, and my interviewer, the Corporate Director of Human Resources, Jay Oswald, appeared to bring me upstairs. The interview was going very well, until Jay asked me what I knew about A.O. Smith Corporation. I sat back, smiled confidently and stated, "Well, I know that A.O. Smith is among the world's leading producers of corn syrup." Jay, who was one of life's great characters and an outstanding HR professional, immediately broke out laughing and said, "Smith, you're obviously lost. You think you're in Decatur, Illinois, talking to A.E. Staley. Here's a news flash! You're in Milwaukee, Wisconsin talking to A.O. Smith, the world's largest producer of car and truck frames!" Needless to say, the distance between truck/car frames and corn syrup is about as far as it is from Milwaukee to Decatur. How did I respond? I said, "Jay, now I really do feel stupid. I drove all the way up here thinking A.E. Staley was based in Milwaukee!" Jay just loved that response and after I admitted that I had not done my homework, he gave me special dispensation for being an idiot! I apologized for my lack of preparation and promised that during our next meeting, that I'd be very well prepared. I <u>was</u> very well prepared for the next meeting with the division's CEO, was ultimately hired, and thoroughly enjoyed my experience as a Human Resources Director for the world's largest manufacturer of car and truck frames. However, I got very, very lucky. Had Jay been a more rigid individual or less experienced, I probably would have been rejected for being so poorly prepared (and for being arrogant to boot!). In a highly competitive job market, this type of error can easily spell your doom as a candidate. The message I'm sending is: know your prospective company as well as you do your own resume. So how do you do this?

To be direct, you must research your prospective company thoroughly. You should know these basic facts about every firm for which you intend to interview:

1. Their correct name! (Just kidding, no one would be dumb enough to begin an interview with the wrong company in mind, would they?)

2. Their primary product/s and/or services.

3. The firm's annual sales for the past 3 years and percentage growth.

4. Degree of profitability, expressed as a percentage of sales and a comparison of that percentage to their competition.

5. The firm's major competitors and how they "stack up" against them.

6. Simple financial measures (ROA, EBITA, debt level—short and long-term debt to assets, etc.).

7. Stock performance over past 12 months (not specific dollar amounts per se, but percentage of gain/loss).

8. Any "scuttlebutt" about the company's culture, environment, pay, benefits, etc. Later, we'll discuss a means of "verifying" that information through asking a series of prepared questions during the course of your meeting.

9. Any "latest news" about the company that has appeared in the business/financial press. Hint: Try a Google search on "press releases".

In this age of the Internet, it is inexcusable to come to an interview without the answers to these questions.

Furthermore, wouldn't you want to thoroughly research any "product" before you make a major "purchase" decision? This type (and more) of information is readily available for virtually every publicly-traded company on a multitude of financial web sites:

www.fidelity.com, googlefinance.com, www.thomson.com, www.yahoo.com, etc.

Even small or privately-held companies can usually be researched by doing a search on Google, Yahoo, Bing, Hoover's Online, etc. If you want to get really serious, access the Securities and Exchange Commission's Edgar site (http://www.sec.gov/edgar.shtml). Edgar is filled with financial information on all publicly-traded companies, including filings, 10-K's, 8-K's, etc. You can also check The Great Places to Work Institute's site to determine whether your prospective employer is listed (or has been listed over the past 4 years). You can also use this site to review what it takes to be considered a great company. The site, located at http://www.greatplacetowork.com, is a great forum for this type of data. Finally, for a bit of real insight, try Vault.com and Glassdoor.com community message boards. Both Vault.com and Glassdoor.com are not only a great place to post your resume and explore job postings, but they are also a terrific venue for getting the "inside scoop" on a prospective employer. On the

"Community" Bulletin Boards, employees (both past and present) and candidates post their experiences and comments about specific companies—and, I might add, they're not exactly bashful about offering up their opinions. You can gain a better understanding of a company's culture, hiring practices, etc. by following the "threads" on the boards. The message boards are arranged alphabetically (i.e. to find AT&T, just click on the "A"), and there are literally hundreds of companies—both large and small—that have postings. Just bear in mind that what you are reading is only one person's opinion and not necessarily an objective and full accounting of the facts behind any event.

You can find Vault at: http://www.vault.com
and Glassdoor at: http://www.glassdoor.com.

Like Vault and Glassdoor, other great sources of information (although sometimes only consisting of gossip, hyperbole and conjecture!) are newsgroups and blogs. I use these forums in my own practice! You'd be surprised what you can find out listening to the comments of others. Again, you have to put on the heavy "filters" when you glean this type of data, but it can be useful to have as you prepare for your interview.

In summary, do your homework . . . *then*, take the test!

COMING PREPARED TO ASK "COMPLEX" QUESTIONS

As I've sat through many interviews, I've noticed two distinct types of candidates with regard to their ability to ask questions.

Type I is the candidate who invariably asks such challenging questions as: "Can you tell me about your benefit plan?", or "Why is this position open?", or "Does this position lead to senior management?", or the ever-popular, "Does this position offer stock options?"

Type II is the candidate who asks, "What are the challenges that you'd expect I'd face in my first 6 months in this role?", or "How would you describe the culture of your company?", or "What competitive threats does your company face?", or "Have you considered candidates from within the company for this position?"

I think you see the difference in the level of demonstrated aggressiveness, intellectual curiosity and potential for further growth in the two candidates. In reality, they may have the same potential and ability, but it is the Type II candidate that gets me excited. The

Type II candidate shows me that they've come to the interview prepared, with the intent of seriously weighing our opportunity against others. The Type II candidate asks the types of questions that generate the greatest amount of data. As a result, a Type II candidate is better able to make a rational, informed decision regarding an offer when it comes. If a Type II candidate receives and accepts our offer, I am more confident that they'll be able to "live" with that decision longer (that is, longer job tenure) because they "knew what they were getting themselves into". I also know that if I refer a Type II candidate on for further interviews, that my hiring managers are going to be equally excited for the same reasons. They'll know that they are interviewing a candidate of quality.

Furthermore, the best companies will evaluate you as a candidate **not only by the answers you give, but by the questions that you ask**! Reasoned, probing and complex questions asked by a candidate say much about the candidate's intellectual horsepower. Every company wants to hire such people—let's make certain that they see that quality in you.

Beyond this rationale, there is also a very subtle, but exceedingly important advantage that Type II candidates give themselves. By asking good questions, they allow the interviewer to "play the expert". By way of explanation, think of your own personal experience—aren't you always pleased when someone asks you for your opinion, or to render judgment? Doesn't it elevate you as a person when you get asked a question beyond the "usual" and actually get to use *your* intellect to provide an answer? Every one of us loves to be in the position of playing the expert—it's human nature! When candidates ask mundane or "stock" questions, they miss an opportunity to make their interviewers feel good about themselves! They miss an opportunity to build greater rapport with their interviewers. As an aside, most HR professionals are used to being asked questions about benefits, vacations, stock options, etc. I can speak from personal experience (having been an HR professional for 12 years) that those questions never made me feel good about the role I was playing in the process. It was almost as if the candidate didn't feel that I could answer more complex questions—when in fact I could! I can guarantee that if you ask your interviewer challenging questions that "stretch" them beyond the ordinary, you will separate yourself from the pack as a high-impact candidate and build greater rapport with your interviewer—particularly if they are an HR professional.

Okay, sounds good you say, but how do I formulate these types of questions?

Earlier, I provided a list of 20 "pre-interview" questions for you to ask about your own company. You can use that same list of questions to ask your interviewers about their company. Each question is designed to generate significant data about the firm and its culture and the way they do business. Most of the 20 questions are not typically asked by candidates on an interview. Consequently, the interviewer is going to mentally file you away as a memorable candidate. Additionally, you should be prepared to ask "operational" questions; that is, questions that probe the financial or operating performance of the company. You can develop a list of questions of this type with the information you've gleaned from your "homework"—as we discussed in the previous section. For example, consider asking, "I noticed in your annual report that the company has increased its long-term debt by 20%. What is driving that increase? Is it because of acquisitions, stock buy-back, or investment in new plants or equipment?" Or, "I've noticed that your R&D spending is greater than XYZ Company (a major competitor). What impact do you think that spending will have on the project that I'll be working on?" These are examples of "operational" questions. If you do your homework, you'll be able to ask similar questions— again the type of questions most candidates don't ask. Do so, elevates you to a different level vis-a-vis the competition. You will also "stretch" your interviewer. And as I stated earlier, allowing your interviewer to "play the expert", will help you to build greater rapport with them.

Finally, to make you appear to be an even more outstanding candidate, I would like you to (surprise!) **prepare your list of questions in advance and have them written down**. Then, when during the interview you are asked, "Do you have any questions?", you can whip out your trusty note pad and start firing out your questions. As we will discuss in Sections III and IV, the interview itself is filled with enough tension and pressure—why add to it by feeling put on the spot and having to fumble around for the "right" question to ask? Having your questions prepared in advance will make you appear to be exactly what you are—the best candidate for the role. You will be doing your job as an outstanding candidate and helping your interviewers to "close the circle"!

FINAL THOUGHTS ON YOUR PRE-INTERVIEW PREPARATION: ARE WE AS TOUGH AS WE THINK WE ARE?

Despite having completed every exercise that I've offered; despite doing thorough "homework" regarding a prospective employer (operating performance, culture, environment, etc.); despite understanding the "boss side of the equation"; despite knowing the likelihood of future prospects for personal and professional growth within the firm; despite knowing all of these things, I find candidates still continue to make poor decisions regarding employment. That is, they continue to accept offers with firms or work for people that they know in advance are the antithesis of their own personal and professional value system. And, they pay the full price for those decisions by having to leave their new firm after only a short period of time—sometimes of their own accord and sometimes as a result of a lay-off or termination caused by what the company terms a "poor fit". Amazing isn't it? The fact is that even with the careful preparation given in this book, people can still make poor career choices. I should know—I've done so myself! The unfortunate reality is that some people continue to make poor decisions over and over again. You only have to look at their resumes and observe a series of 12-month, 15-

month and 9-month jobs in succession to realize that something is afoot!

You might ask, why do these otherwise highly intelligent and capable people defy the facts in plain view, eliminate logic, and ignore their own good judgment so as to make worthless the extensive research, effort, and preparation they've invested in making a correct employment decision? As important, why do people make this identical mistake again and again? As a way of explaining this phenomenon let me take a moment to share a real event that took place a few years ago.

I was working with a candidate—we'll call him Rick. Rick was a Director of HR at a manufacturing division of a Fortune 100 company. He had been on an extremely fast track throughout his career and had achieved real success. He had an MM (now MBA) from Northwestern University's Kellogg School and had an undergraduate in Industrial Relations from a Big 10 university, where he also had been on a full athletic scholarship and a 2-year football defensive starter.

During our meeting, among other attributes, I could tell that Rick's family was very important to him and that he placed a high value on the amount of time he was able to spend with them. Rick was also a consensus builder—he liked working in a team environment, where through collaboration everybody wins.

Through me, he received an offer as a VP Human Resources with a high growth, high-tech firm. The company's culture and environment, boss relationship, and work-life balance were very well suited to his own value system. However, despite all of these positives, he rejected that offer to accept another offer, from a different search firm, as a Manager of HR at a Fortune 20 corporation. This role would require him to live apart from his family until the end of the school year when they would be able to join him in his new location. Additionally, from what I knew of this firm's culture, I knew there would be many other disconnects for Rick as well. When I asked him to explain the rationale behind his decision, he indicated that the Fortune 20 firm's compensation was slightly better and that despite the title of "Manager" vs. VP, the roles were very comparable—given the significantly larger size and scope of the Fortune 20 firm. He stated that he knew in advance that he would have to work more hours at the Fortune 20 firm, including weekends. He also indicated that he would be entering a very tough work environment created by the firm's hard, unforgiving culture. But, he said, these were not the overriding factors in his decision. He stated that even though he was aware of all of these potential negatives as a result of his interviewing experience, he was accepting their offer because, "Gary, I've got to see if I can play with the best!" Knowing that his mind was made up, I could only wish him the best of luck and ask that he stay in touch.

Five months later, I received a phone call from Rick. He indicated that he was leaving his new company and returning to Chicago to begin another job search, and asked if I would I help him in that effort. Bear in mind, I really liked this guy and wanted to help him, but I had to ask, "What happened?" His story in explanation was instructive. He responded by saying:

"I should have known, even from the first interview that this was going to be all wrong for me. Everything I felt would be a problem on the interview, turned out to be even worse once I got there. I was working 15 hours a day. Saturdays meant at least 5 hours. I would get conference calls on Sunday evenings. I was literally on call 24/7. I never saw my family, even when they moved to join me. The culture was brutal and highly political. The level of profanity used by everyone was incredible! There were shouting matches daily and if you didn't push back just as hard, you were lost. The company demanded perfection and high performance and didn't tolerate any excuses."

He continued by telling me about an event that took place on his final round of interviews that "should have told me all I needed to know." He stated on that round of interviews, he had first met with the Division Director of HR—his boss to be. After a 1-hour meeting, he left the Director's office thinking that his potential new boss was intelligent, polite and respectful—a good start. Rick then proceeded to interview with 5 other managers representing both the HR and line organizations. After his last interview, he was taken back to his starting point, the Director, Human Resource's office—however, the door was closed. Because it was apparent that some sort of meeting was taking place, Rick was asked to sit in a chair outside of the door and wait. As he sat there he could hear a highly vocal argument taking place—albeit one that was very much one-sided. Someone was obviously getting "drilled"—by the volume level and amount of profanity being used. Rick indicated that at this point, he was thinking that maybe this new boss was a more problematic individual than he appeared. Maybe he was a lot tougher to work for and maybe it wasn't such a good idea to work for this man after all. In the midst of this thought process the door was flung open and out stormed the division President—his boss' boss. He then realized that it was not his potential boss who had been doing the yelling and screaming, but instead his potential boss had been on the <u>receiving</u> end.

Rick said, "At that point I should have realized that this was not the right place for me to be! I thought I could learn to like their culture. I sure wanted to try—because I wanted to be tested by the best."

A lesson learned to be sure.

So again, why do people make such decisions with regard to matters that have such serious consequences—even though they innately know the decision to be the wrong one? Every one of us can relate to this scenario easily as every one of us has made at least one poor choice in our lives. And, most likely, we made that poor choice even though our minds and "gut" told us to decide otherwise.

I'd like to answer this question by giving you an example of this human tendency at work. It appears in the movie classic, *The Sting*, winner of the Academy Award for Best Picture in 1973. *The Sting* starred Paul Newman and Robert Redford at the height of their careers. It was a casting reunion of sorts after their success in *Butch Cassidy and the Sundance Kid*. In the film, Redford plays a talented, but brash confidence man, Johnny Hooker, in 1920's Chicago. He seeks revenge against the very tough and murderous Chicago gangster, Doyle Lonnegan, played by the late, great Robert Shaw (perhaps best known for his role as Captain Quint in *Jaws*). Newman portrayed the wise and experienced con man, Harry Gondorf, who was considered the master of the high-end "sting"—that is, a swindle used to con rich people out of their money. Redford's character, Hooker, had sworn to "get" Lonnegan as revenge for having Hooker's best friend killed when a con they were running inadvertently ripped off one of Lonnegan's men. As the movie progresses, Newman takes Redford's character to Chicago's Union Station to identify and size up Lonnegan, who will be their "mark" for this high-end sting. As Lonnegan walks past, Newman points him out to Redford, who, seeing him for the first time, says, "He's not as tough as he thinks he is!" Newman gives Redford a wise look and says, "Neither are we, kid!"

These lines spoken by Newman's and Redford's characters at the end of this scene were quite humorous. But in reality, they underscore our very human tendency in decision-making; that is, to cast a blind eye to reality and assume that we're capable of overcoming any obstacle that gets in our path. This "blind spot" is particularly evident in high-performing people who have known great success. As human beings, we tend to assess the problems that we will face in a new company/job and underestimate or even ignore them! We are sublimely confident that we can overcome any obstacle (poor financial position of company, failing products or markets, bad boss equation, destructive corporate culture, etc.) based on our past success. The fact remains that some companies and jobs have problems that cannot be overcome by any single person—regardless of their ability! Unfortunately, it is also this very type of company that often pushes our "ego" button. Our ego tells us that we will succeed despite any and all obstacles in our path! So we accept the offer and the "no-win" scenario attached to it.

My advice is, when faced with this choice, listen to objective reality, know when to just say "no", and pass. Remember, none of us is as tough as we think we are.

At this point in the process, having completed all four exercises, having retooled your resume into a high-impact, selling document, and having considered the many other key elements in the pre-interview thought process, you probably think that you know yourself and your capabilities pretty well. Well, that may be the case. But just how well do you know your "Digital Self"—that is, what's "out there" about you . . . on the Internet? As you read on, I think you'll agree that cleaning up your digital act—in today's job market—is an essential element in job hunting success. So, exactly what do I mean by "cleaning up your digital act"?

CLEANING UP YOUR DIGITAL ACT

While in college, I have to admit to having been somewhat less than a total gentleman. I did some outrageous things "back in the day" most of which I'm glad to have left very far behind me and buried in the deep past. With the exception of getting together with a few fraternity brothers and reminiscing about the old days, no one is aware or tuned in to the mistakes of my past. Unfortunately, this is not so, with today's Facebook, Twitter, and YouTube generation. In short, if you've posted, or had posted by someone else, any compromising pictures, videos, blogs, emails, chats or statements—on-line—then, they are now sitting there waiting, like a ticking time bomb, ready to explode your chances of a new job.

Would it surprise you to learn that according to the Ponemon Institute, one of the nation's premier privacy and information management research firms (www.ponemon.org) that 61% of companies routinely perform on-line background checks before extending job offers? And, here's something else to consider—just slightly under half of those firms decided against hiring a candidate based on what they "learned" on-line. In other words, what they learned from an on-line search actually caused an offer to disappear!

According to Careerbuilder.com, when hiring managers (or HR) checked out candidates on-line they found that:

- 31% lied about their backgrounds or qualifications
- 43% were either linked to some form of criminality or bragged about their drinking or drug-taking prowess
- 11% posted provocative pictures of themselves—and, I'll let you guess what I mean by "provocative")
- Etc., etc., etc.

What this means to you—as a job seeker—is that you have to be very careful indeed about what you post about yourself and what others post about you. Certainly, you don't want all of your hard work through every step of the job search process to be flushed away by the outcome of that Beer Pong game you had as an undergraduate! Now, I'm not suggesting that you live the life of a monk, or in a cloister—only that you exercise reasonable precautions about what is "out there"; and, to make every effort to fix what already is.

As an aside, while I personally could care less about an individual's "private" behavior, I do know that there are many companies that do care and will make decisions based on that behavior. In a perfect world, private behavior would be considered out-of-bounds and untouchable, but we both know that the world is quite a bit less than perfect. Rather than rail against the injustice of companies having the temerity to investigate your personal life, when considering you professionally, face up to and accept the fact that it happens and it is the way it is—we're not going to change it. Companies feel they have the right to make a hiring decision based on the "whole candidate"—that is, a synthesis of the individual's professional and personal background. Simply put, companies think that what you do on your personal time can reflect on your professional judgment and credibility. As a result, the time to make changes and adjustments to your digital self is sooner, not later.

To fix this potential problem, start with a simple Google search on your name. See what pops up. Next, perform that same search and start adding new search parameters—such as your fraternity or sorority, your school/s, companies, organizations, etc. Use different search engines to perform these searches, as each engine (Google, Yahoo, Bing, etc.) performs its search in a slightly different manner (e.g. different algorithms).

If you have a Facebook account, make your profile "private". Check out your "wall" and remove compromising pictures and posts. If you are a "LinkedIn" user or a member of any other professional networking group, make certain that what is posted matches up perfectly against your resume (i.e. make sure dates, jobs, etc. are in alignment).

One last consideration is your choice of "screen names" or email addresses. If you have a screen handle of "hotpantsgirl" on-line, or have an email address of "drinksitallguy@whatever.com", you're probably not going to be taken very seriously by your prospective employer. Again, be proactive—take the necessary steps to fix a potential problem in advance of your search—not during or after.

This sounds very interesting, you say, but how much trouble can I really get into because of what's out there on the internet? Let me tell you a story . . .

About a year ago, I was conducting a search for a Vice President, Human Resources for a $5B+ manufacturing company on the West Coast. As I was putting my candidate slate together, I uncovered a candidate who looked great on paper. The candidate, we'll call her Leslie, had a terrific background—undergraduate degree from first-tier school, MBA from a Top 10, and a law degree from a second-tier school. Looking at her resume you would have been impressed—she had worked for all the right companies, had good job stability and had made the right moves at the right time. According to her resume, she was the incumbent VP of HR for a high-tech division of a major company. We'll call this company Attitude, Inc.—a company that you would definitely know. All in all, she looked great on paper! I called her and had a preliminary talk and liked her even more! She was also fully bi-lingual (English/Spanish) which was one of the items on my client's wish list. At that point, I did a quick Google search on her and checked her LinkedIn profile—everything came back clean. I then called her company's main number and asked for her. Please note that I do this for only those candidates about whom I'm really serious. You might ask, why would I call her company on the main number and not the "office number" the candidate gave me? This is an attempt to make certain that the candidate is really working for the company they say they are. Sure enough, I asked for Leslie and was put through, reaching her voice mail. So far, so good.

As the process went forward, our 2 finalists turned out to be Leslie and another candidate, Bob. My client was leaning towards Leslie and asked me to begin the reference check process. At that point I performed another Google search—just 3 weeks after the one I'd done initially—and lo and behold—trouble in River City. In that second search, I uncovered a press release indicating that Leslie has just been appointed SVP Human Resources with a software company based in the Western U.S. According to the appointment date on the press release, Leslie had begun her employment with the new company about 2 weeks before I had made initial contact with her. Suffice to say, this revelation came as a total shock to me as I had had multiple conversations with her, including a 90-minute in-depth interview, and she had never mentioned that she had left Attitude—in fact, quite the contrary, she was talking about how hard it would be for her to leave in a timely fashion, given the number of projects in which she was involved. So, what did your favorite recruiter do next? I called the software company and asked for Leslie. To my further surprise, I found that she was no longer working at that company! In fact, she had left abruptly the preceding Friday after a run-in with her boss, the CEO. Both of these items really piqued my curiosity. With my suspicions aroused, I then gave her references a call. The output of her reference check was twofold—first, that she really was an outstanding HR professional and second, that she had omitted 2 more jobs (a 3-month and a 6 month) from her resume—over and above her most recent cover-up. I called my client, gave them the report and we immediately went to Plan B and hired Bob.

As a footnote to this story, I did call Leslie and very politely approached her with my findings, and explained that because of the discrepancies in her background, my client would not be offering her the position. Can you believe that she got angry and accused me of being unprofessional? How dare I investigate her! Was I calling her a liar? ("Um, yes, I was!") She angrily stated that, "My word should have been good enough!" Anything you've heard is all lies!" etc., etc., etc. It never ceases to amaze me how there is that type of person, who when confronted with their deceit and lies, has the audacity to attempt to spin it and put the onus on you. I guess it is just another example of the broad range of behaviors in the human condition.

The moral to this story should be clear. Even if you are totally "clean" with regard to "compromising behavior" on the internet, make certain that was is "factually" stated about you is, in fact, factual. If it is, then it's your responsibility to make certain that your resume is in complete alignment with the paper trail that exists on the internet.

In sum, the importance of cleaning up your digital act cannot be over-stressed. Before beginning your job search, you'll need to know what's "out there" and either remove or change it, or bring your own presentation into alignment with it.

Caveat Applicantus!

SECTION III -- "TOOLS" OF THE INTERVIEWING TRADE

Up to this point we've discussed the philosophy and principals of interviewing and career success. We've gained greater insight into our preferences regarding culture and environment in organizations. We have developed a personal Success Matrix which articulates our plan. In other words, we have completed the preparation necessary to enter into the interview process. Picture this section then, "Tools of the Interviewing Trade", as a toolkit for interview success.

These tools will specifically address common interview distractions or faux pas that candidates can make during the interview process. Revisiting the list of "Why Candidates Fail on Interviews" on page 28, we know that candidate rejection can occur for any number of reasons—most of which have nothing to do with the actual functional capability of the candidate. My goal is for you to be evaluated based on your interview performance and capabilities—not based on trivial or spurious data. Consider this next section a compendium of problems and their solutions that addresses many of the issues identified on the "Why Candidates Fail" list.

Please note, that some of the ideas expressed in this section will make it appear that I am attempting to play the role of the psychiatrist or psychologist—believe me, nothing could be further from my intent. I am not qualified to be "that guy". However, after you've interviewed 10,000+ candidates over the years, you do get a sense of what works and what doesn't. As a result, what follows is a toolkit developed from the actual interview experiences of my candidates. You may not need every tool in this section, but I'm confident that there will be several that will help you improve your overall interview batting average—particularly, with the dreaded "telephone screen"!

THE TELEPHONE INTERVIEW/SCREEN

I just referred to the telephone interview as the "Dreaded Telephone Screen". My primary reason for identifying this often-necessary step in the recruiting process as "dreaded" is that I am <u>not</u> a big fan of telephone "screening" interviews. In my opinion, it is like going into a final exam with an "A" grade . . . you can, typically, only lower your score. This same modality is at work on the telephone screen as there are about 7 things that can happen on the telephone interview—6 are bad, 1 is good. Here are some examples:

1. Interview times are not kept. This is very common — so prepare yourself. You'll wait by the phone at the appointed time and the phone won't ring. And, you'll continue to wait the rest of the day/evening until it is very apparent that the call is just not going to happen. Sure enough, the next day, you'll get a call from your recruiter (if you're working with one) indicating that "something came up" and that the company would like to reschedule. Don't be offended if this happens. In my own experience, unless I'm really riding herd over my client, this happens about 70% of the time. In other words, without the specter of a real, live human being waiting in a lobby or office, it's easy for day-to-day events in the life of the telephone interviewer to cause the call to be late or even not happen. Regardless, I know it can be frustrating to you, as a candidate, to be "all dressed up and nowhere to go". However, sometimes it's just the nature of the beast.

Let me stress, though, that while one disconnect is permissible, a second is an indication of something amiss within the company's process. Let's face it, if something is truly important, you'll make the time. If the call keeps getting rescheduled, it may be an indication of just how important the company's interviewer views this role and/or you as a candidate.

2. If the screening call is being made by the HR representative or worse, a "contract recruiter", you may find yourself talking with someone who is woefully under-informed about the position's requirements and candidate profile. In this scenario you will be attempting to "sell" yourself to an individual who may have only a passing knowledge of the actual role and its responsibilities and instead, may just be screening you against a list of pre-determined criteria. In other words, if you "check all the boxes" perfectly, no problem. However, if your interviewer lacks a complete understanding of the actual nature of the work, you may have difficulty connecting your experience to the "checkboxes" the screener is attempting to fill

in. This can result in you, as a perfectly good candidate, being screened out.

3. In most cases, you'll not be the only "screening" interview the company's representative is performing. Imagine that you are the recruiter making the call and that you have been on the phone for the past 3 hours making 20 minute "phone screens". This can burn out even the best recruiter. If you find yourself being screened by a person already in this mode, it can be very difficult to succeed as a candidate. For this reason, I always suggest that you immediately engage your interviewer with an empathy-building line such as, "I'm guessing I'm not the first person you've been talking with today!" When you get the expected, "No, I've had a few today.", then do the right thing and acknowledge the difficult nature of the recruiter's job by stating, "I have to believe that it's tough to make that many calls", or words to that effect. Your intent is to build rapport with your screener, and as always, make yourself memorable—in a positive way. It doesn't cost you anything to acknowledge the hard work of others, and you

may find yourself accruing major returns for minimal effort in terms of your screener's willingness to pass you on to the next stage in the process.

4. Remember, as we discussed in a previous section, the "mission" of many HR professionals is to screen you out, not to screen you in. Always bear this in mind when you interview over the phone. Treat any phone interview as an even tougher venue than a face-to-face meeting.

5. Over the phone, an inexperienced interviewer loses so much of the real candidate. Without substantial experience performing telephone interviews, the interviewer typically relies on "gut feeling" or presumption—and both are equally dangerous to you as a candidate. This is because with such limited data, they tend to formulate conclusions on small things—things, that in a face-to-face interview, would not be a significant or even considered part of the equation. The next item is related to this.

6. In a telephone screening interview, it is very easy, as a candidate, to talk too much, or say

inappropriate things that lead to rejection. Again, in a face-to-face interview, a candidate can see/hear the verbal and non-verbal cues that the interviewer is sending in response to what they're saying--and change directions before falling into a black hole. Over the phone, without the visual, this is lost.

7. The good news, though, is that because telephone interviews are short (15-30 minutes), they tend to be straightforward and to the point. Because a screening interview is not the time or place to conduct a thorough interview with behaviorally-oriented questions, you can usually predict the questions to be asked. They are:

    - "Tell me about yourself." OR "Walk me through your background."

    - "Why would you leave your current position?" OR "Why did you leave (previous companies)?"

    - "What type of position are you looking for?"

- "What are you currently earning?" AND "What type of compensation are you interested in?"

However, I'd also like you to consider that there may be specific questions that may be asked— designed to fill in the "boxes" on the screener's checklist. For example, let's suppose that you're being screened for a Sales Management role. You might be asked questions such as:

- "Give me an example of a tough negotiation and how you handled it."

- "Give me an example of a difficult client experience and how you handled it."

- "Tell me about the things you like to do. Tell me about the thing you don't like to do."

- "Can you give me an example of a successful selling experience? How about one that was not successful? How did you handle both?"

These questions were probably given to the screener by the hiring manager as being "knock outs"; that is, you'll have to give the "right" answers to move forward in the process. These questions can also give you an indication as to the true nature of the role and the likely direction a "face-to-face" interview will take. If you've done your homework you should be in a position to answer these questions effectively.

So, how can you improve your chances to succeed on a telephone interview or "screen"? Here's what I'm going to highly recommend you do:

1. Do your homework! A.) Study the firm's website and take written notes. B.) Re-read the position description. C.) Remember your conversations with your recruiter, if applicable, as they described the job and its mission and the culture of the company. Integrate these 3 elements into your preparation and understanding.

2. Rehearse the questions above and be prepared to answer them

succinctly. Remember, in a telephone interview, if you ramble, you lose!

3. Prepare a list of questions in advance and have them written out. If you want to be an "A" candidate, then you have to act like one. In most cases, the time element associated with a telephone screening interview will simply not allow the screener to spend too much time on your questions. However, in the event you're asked, you want to be prepared. Simply, "winging it" when it's your turn to ask questions, makes it look like you're winging it. Think about it . . . how professional can anyone appear when they get their chance to ask questions and they ask, "Uh . . . why is the job open?" I think you get the picture. Remember, asking the type of questions that make you look thoughtful and like you've done your homework beforehand, is essential to making a positive impression in a 15-30 minute phone interview.

4. Seriously consider the business impact (positive, of course) that you've had on your company/ies. Be prepared to articulate this in your responses.

5. Most important . . . be yourself! Relax, be positive and enthusiastic, have fun and remember to engage your interviewer. If you get too serious about the telephone screen, you'll come across as stilted and robotic. Remember, the person on the other end of phone can't see you. They don't know that you're a really great individual and have an equally great sense of humor. You don't have to be a comedian, but you don't want to come off as a stiff, either. Strike a balance and again, just be yourself!

6. Remember, as we discussed earlier, the "mission" of many HR professionals is to screen you out---not screen you in. So, while the HR professional can sound friendly and engaging, they also have a mission. Always be aware of what that mission is.

Best of luck, and don't forget to have fun! Maybe it won't be so dreaded after all!

MORE PRE-INTERVIEW PREPARATION: 7 KEYS TO INTERVIEW SUCCESS

Over the years, I've coached thousands of candidates in the necessary preparation for their interviews. Recently, I got tired (after 30 years it can happen!) of repeating myself before every interview, so designed a quick overview of the homework that I expect every candidate to complete prior to their interviews. I call it, the "7 Keys to Interview Success":

1. "Vet" your interviewer's LinkedIn profile in advance of your meeting—getting to know your interviewer in advance takes some of the "pressure" off of the meeting.

2. Do your homework! Really hit the company's website so you know the company's locations, services, customers, etc. Also, perform a Google search for other relevant information (press releases, new product introductions, key personnel changes, etc.).

3. Arrive 10 minutes ahead of your scheduled interview time so that you can use the facilities, get oriented, complete the employment

application, etc. If you're going to be late for whatever reason, call your interviewer and give them a "heads-up".

4. Bring your business card.

5. Bring a notebook/portfolio to take notes—and actually take notes during your meeting!

6. Come to the meeting with your questions prepared and written in advance.

7. Wait until first thing the morning after your interview, send a "Thank You" email to your interview/s. I counsel you to wait until the morning after, because most candidates send that "Thank You" email, immediately after the interview. In doing so, the action appears to be automatic and reflexive—as in: "Well, they expect me to send a note, so I better do it!" I recommend to my candidates that you send that "Thank You" email the morning after, because doing so makes you appear "thoughtful". It's a subtle difference, but it's also part of the image and perceptions that we are crafting. More on this follows in a later section of this book.

CONTROLLING NERVOUSNESS

Everyone is nervous to some degree before a job interview. Believe it or not, very often interviewers themselves are nervous before or during an interview—particularly if the position being recruited for is a senior level role with high visibility, or if the interviewer is inexperienced. Why do people get nervous? After all, it's only an interview. It's not like your career, your house, your financial future, choice of your children's colleges, etc., hang on the outcome of an interview!

Seriously, nervousness hovers over an interview for two reasons. First, we want people to like us—that's just human nature. In any interview situation, there is a chance that we might not be "liked" and might be rejected. Second, an employment interview, for most people, is not something they do every day. Very few people are "professional interviewees." In the uncharted territory of the interview, most candidates don't know what to expect or how to formulate, in advance, how they should act and react. It is this "element of the unknown" that is a major contributor to increased stress and nervousness. This is one of the reasons why we go to such lengths to prepare for the interview, so as to minimize as many of the unknown elements as possible and thus reduce our nervousness. Approaching every interview in a more confident, relaxed manner is a direct output of being fully prepared.

Can anyone be nervous before an interview? Of course! Everyone gets nervous to some degree before a major presentation—even some of the greatest speakers and presenters will admit to having "opening night jitters" before a big presentation. As an example, considered to be among the greatest statesmen and orators in history is Marcus Tullius Cicero (109-43 BC) of the late Republican period of Rome. In Republican Rome, having the ability to speak persuasively in public was an irreplaceable skill if one were to achieve dominance and power in public life. As a consequence, there were many outstanding orators in Rome. However, even the great Julius Caesar was considered only the second-best orator of his day— second to the abilities of Cicero. Cicero held a hugely influential place in Roman politics—primarily because of his abilities as a public speaker. However, even Cicero got nervous before a presentation. In fact, he admitted:

"Personally, I am always nervous when I begin to speak. Every time I make a speech I feel that I am submitting to judgment, not only about my ability, but my character and honor." (Cicero, In Defense of Cluentius—*Pro Cluentio*)

So . . . if a Marcus Tullius Cicero can get nervous, it's only natural if you do, too. However, our goal should be to positively channel that energy and not allow it to become a destructive force.

THE "NIGHT BEFORE" AND THE MORNING OF YOUR INTERVIEW

It is now the night before your interview. You have completed your homework—now you're ready to take the test. However, most of us are a bit "keyed-up" the night before our interviews. There is definitely a certain amount of stress and pressure associated with an interview because of our innate need to be "liked", the importance of succeeding and the uncertainty of the outcome. Don't forget, that for most people, being subjected to public scrutiny is not something they do every day. And further, if you're unemployed (or about to be), there's even more riding on your upcoming meeting. Therefore, it is very understandable if you're a bit tense the night before the event. For me to ask you not to be nervous is probably a futile request. Instead, let's discuss how you should complete your preparation the "night before" and the morning of your interview so as to best manage whatever pre-interview stress you might feel. Completing these small, but important tasks will have the effect of minimizing your "stress level" just prior to your meeting.

"DRESS" THE NIGHT BEFORE

Rather than run around in the morning of your interview frantically searching for that particular matching tie or purse, select and "lay-out" your interview clothing the night before the interview. If your shoes need to be shined do it the night before. If your car needs gas, fill it up the night before. If you are uncertain of the location of your interview, determine the correct route the night before. A visit to Google Maps or your phone's GPS works wonders! I personally like to use the "satellite" view on Google Maps and see the "birds-eye" view of the building or site. It gives me a better sense of the surrounding area. The idea is to eliminate anything that might slow you down or distract you the morning of your interview.   As we've already discussed (and will discuss again in detail in the next section) most people are a bit nervous (or quite a bit nervous) just prior to their interviews. Our objective in this instance is to remove any potential cause of added stress and allow you to focus on the matter at hand. On the morning of the interview, you'll want to have only one thing on your mind— that is, mentally preparing yourself for your interview—not attempting to ascertain the location of your only pair of clean black socks.

VISUALIZATION, AFFIRMATION AND SLEEP

I have spoken with many candidates who have indicated that they were "so charged up" the night before the interview, they found it hard to sleep. They "just couldn't wait to get going!" Unfortunately, lack of sleep is counter-productive to your cause. You want to allow ample sleep time so that you wake up feeling and looking rested. To be at your best on the interview, you'll need sleep.

I suggest that as you prepare to sleep, first, visualize yourself in the interview—smiling and facing your interviewer with confidence. Second, affirm to yourself that the company considers you an excellent prospect—after all, it was the company that chose to bring you in for the interview. Third, know that your proven experience will be an invaluable asset to the firm. Having considered these thoughts, clear your mind and sleep!

THE MORNING OF YOUR INTERVIEW

The only counsel I can offer for the morning of your interview is to allocate enough time to get to the interview in a timely fashion. You'll want to be in the lobby ready to be "announced" 5 minutes prior to your scheduled appointment. This will allow you adequate time to use the "facilities" and get focused. While in the lobby you can read a book, annual report, etc. subject to the guidelines we'll discuss in the section "Stand or Sit?".

DID DARWIN HAVE SWEATY PALMS?

Now, I know this is going to sound goofy to some of you, but for many folks this topic becomes a real issue when they engage in the handshake ritual that accompanies every introduction between two people. Rather than talk about handshakes (firm, brief, etc.), I thought we'd discuss a troublesome side effect of the handshaking ritual that candidates sometime experience—the "Sweaty Palms Syndrome", or SPS.

For many people this is a by-product of pre-game nervousness, and despite everything they do, they just don't seem to be able to control it. The downside is that when it is time to shake hands, it is difficult for the interviewer to do anything afterwards but wipe their hand down the side of their khakis. As first impressions go, this is probably not the best opener.

Interestingly, SPS is an evolutionary artifact. Our primate ancestors developed this trait as an output of the "fight or flight" reflex generated by fear—usually of a predator. In those times, one could either chose to stand and fight, or take the fastest means of getting out of the danger zone—running away or climbing a tree or rock. Any of these actions required a sudden increase in the level in physical output, that in turn required a corresponding increase in the output of adrenalin, an increase in heart rate and respiration, etc.—the combination of which increased body temperature. Increased perspiration, therefore, was a necessary means of keeping the now highly-energized body cool. Net: perspiration on the palm is nothing more than a natural evolutionary adaptation of our sympathetic nervous system.

A proven method to overcome SPS is to arrive for your meeting early enough (as previously discussed!) to use the men's/ladies room. After freshening up a bit, go to the sink and wash your hands *with soap* and warm water. Then turn on the cold tap only, and let the cold water run over your hands for about a minute. After drying you'll notice that the cold water has closed the pores of your hands which will temporarily halt excessive perspiration. Also, using soap will remove most of the naturally present oil in your skin—which when combined with perspiration makes for the "slimy" feeling that SPS generates. So, the next time you suffer from SPS, try this technique. It works!

STAND OR SIT

Believe it or not, a great time to begin controlling pre-interview nervousness can start when you arrive in the lobby for your interview. Think just a second . . . when you walk into the lobby for your interview, what type of image would you like to project? Would you like to appear as an action-oriented leader—one who is ready to move into action on a moment's notice? Would you like to present yourself so that physically you are in your most attractive state? Would you like to be perceived as a person who controls situations, and does not allow situations to control them? Would you like to appear as someone whose time is valuable and who is not used to being kept waiting? And finally, would you like to create all of these images and at the same time, control your nervousness?

Is there a means of accomplishing all of these things? Let's review a typical scenario:

You are a candidate with a 9:00 AM interview with the HR Representative. You walk into the reception lobby, introduce yourself to the receptionist, give her your name and inform her that you have an appointment to meet with Ms. Habersham, the HR Representative. The receptionist, smiles, picks up the phone and announces your arrival to Ms. Habersham, and then motions for you to have a seat. You walk over to the seating area, see the overstuffed couches or wing chairs that are present in every lobby, and sit down. Good so far?

Now, most of us know that lobby couches are designed to make people feel very comfortable— during the omnipresent wait in the lobby prior to their meeting. In other words, it is *expected* that you will have to wait prior to your meeting. So, let's continue . . . you're sitting down and getting "comfortable" . . . what happens then?

You sit in the chair, and the minutes go by. You try not to squirm and fidget, but you are getting more nervous as the seconds pass. In the meantime, because you are so "comfortable", the receptionist, having done her job, is able to dismiss you mentally and go back to what she was doing. And you wait, and wait, and wait. The longer you wait, the more nervous energy is building up inside of you. You can't release it because you are sitting in this very comfortable chair. It's now 9:20 and finally, Ms. Habersham comes into the lobby to greet you. At this point, the energy you have stored is enough to launch you into low orbit—and, unless you are applying for a job on the space shuttle, that's probably not where you want to be! Another consideration of sitting in a lobby is the image you project to your interviewer. We've all heard the old saw, "You never get a second chance to make a first impression". So, here you sit, with your knees up in your chest, your suit crumpled, and with "Mission Impossible" facing you—getting up gracefully from the couch. To be sure, Ms. Habersham's first image of you is looking down.

She has the elevated position of dominance all to herself. She's the Alpha dog in the lead and you're just one of the pack. You appear passive and in reaction mode; i.e. you're responding to Ms. Habersham's presence and are at her command. All in all, not a very subliminally favorable first impression of you, is it?

How about this scenario in contrast?

You walk into the reception lobby and announce yourself to the receptionist. She motions you to the couch to sit, you say, "No thanks. It feels good to stand up for a bit." You smile at her and then move to an unobtrusive place in the lobby (but, where she can still see you) and stand and begin to wait. You can look out a window, pick up a magazine or newspaper, etc., but *you don't sit down*. P.S. You don't want to stand right in front of the receptionist— that's going to upset her (i.e. you're not showing "trust" that she'll do her job!) and you're going to lose an opportunity to watch human nature in action.

Be advised that there are four advantages of standing vs. sitting in the lobby while you wait for your interview:

1. When you're standing, you're able to burn off more nervous energy than sitting down.

2. Remember what you looked like sitting in that overstuffed chair or couch? Now contrast that to the image you project in a standing position when the interviewer walks into the lobby to meet you. You can't help but look action-oriented—ready for anything. You are able to keep your clothing looking "pressed" and are physically at your most attractive state. You also have the advantage of not allowing the interviewer to "look down" at you as a first image—this is a subtle, but important edge when starting a meeting.

3. If you stand, it projects the image that you're not used to being kept waiting—hence there has never been a need for you to sit down and "get comfortable." Standing implies that you don't have any experience in being kept waiting, so it never occurs to you that you should sit in a lobby.

4. Finally, and very important, is that when you stand in the lobby, you are denying the

receptionist the ability to ignore you. Most people want to do a great job, and our receptionist friend has that same need. With you standing, she senses that something is not quite right, but she can't quite put her finger on it. She experiences a slight discomfort that only increases as the minutes tick by without your interviewer arriving. What happens next will make you laugh (after all, we have to have some fun with the process don't we?)! If you are kept waiting longer than 10 minutes, you'll notice that the receptionist will pick up the phone, call Ms. Habersham again, and inform her that, "Mr. Smith is *still* in the lobby." Thus, you've caused her to take action on your behalf without saying a word or seeming impatient—which you do not want to be seen as being. Receptionists hate that impatient, jerk candidate who shows displeasure at being kept waiting. And, my experience has been that they invariably report their "findings" to your interviewer!

I have experimented with standing or sitting in lobbies over the past 20 years that I've been an executive recruiter visiting clients. I have found, that virtually 100% of the time, if I stand, I wait significantly less time for my meeting to begin, than if I sit. In fact, I can almost time it down to the second when the receptionist is going to pick up the phone and make that second call. I still marvel at the consistency of human behavior. Try this technique yourself—I know you'll have the same experience.

As an aside, if you are standing and constantly looking at your watch, you remove the "guilt trip" from the receptionist. Instead of her "wanting to make things better for you" (and *herself*, by removing the discomfort she feels with you having to wait) by getting you out of her lobby and into your meeting, you become just another impatient job applicant. At that point she can write you off without feeling that she hasn't been doing her job. The message: If you have to check the time, do so when she's not watching!

SITTING, SPACE AND RELATED BODY LANGUAGE

Most candidates are unaware of the powerful signals they project by the manner in which they sit and move while they're meeting with their interviewer. Have you ever watched a tennis match and observed the body position of a player just before they receive a serve? You'll see them move from side to side as they await the serve, and just prior to receiving, they'll get up on their toes—some even bounce up and down. The same is true in baseball, where just prior to the pitch, an infielder who has been flat-footed, will get into a crouch and up on his toes—ready and able to move to either side instantly based upon where the ball is hit. In both cases, the athletes are in an "action-oriented" position. Great athletes do this. Great candidates use action-oriented body language in the way they sit during the interview and the image they project. As in the lobby, we want to appear as though we are in control of events versus responding to them.

I know what you're thinking, now this guy is going to tell me how to sit in a chair! Heck, that is so basic—everyone knows how to sit in a chair.

I make this point because as a veteran of 10,000+ interviews, I can speak from personal experience about the number of candidates who utilize terrible posture and body language when doing something as basic as sitting in a chair during the interview. The numbers would amaze you!

To create the perception of an action-oriented, professional person, sit up straight in your chair, making certain that your lower back is placed firmly against the back of the chair at its base. Hands should be kept in your lap or better, resting at ease on the arms of the chair in a position to gesture when trying to emphasize a point. Your back should be straight, with your upper body inclined slightly towards the interviewer. I am not attempting to convey that you should sit like a statue, only that "chair slouch" is a common form of "relaxing" on the interview and to be avoided.

Under no circumstances should you put your hands, arms, elbows, etc. on the interviewer's desk. Also, with the exception of a drink (resting on a coaster), none of your personal items should be on the interviewer's desk (no purses, portfolios, glasses, papers, etc.). It's the interviewer's desk and "space"—not yours! Your personal items should be placed in the chair beside you or on the floor directly to the side of your chair. Many interviewers begin to feel uncomfortable if you use their desk as your own—and will begin to produce non-verbal cues signaling their discomfort. For example, you might notice the interviewer move his chair further away from you, or he may lose eye contact with you, or pick up an object and place it between you—all of these actions have the effect of the interviewer putting you at a greater distance.

The interviewer's desk should be used by a candidate only if invited to do so by the interviewer. For example, sometimes it is necessary to refer to a paper on the interviewer's desk and point to various areas on the paper. In this case it is just fine to stand up and come alongside the interviewer's desk (leaning over the desk makes you look like a customer talking to a banker in an open lobby—i.e. a supplicant—get the picture?) and with a pen or pencil, point to the area in question on the paper. This is preferable to using your finger to point for aesthetic reasons.

EYE CONTACT

Regarding eye contact, consider this: when we are talking with someone, we like to be looked at. Having eye contact with a person gives them the feeling that you are listening to them and that they are at the center of your universe. However, during interviews, candidates sometimes lose or do not maintain regular eye contact with the interviewer—often with negative consequences.

I am reminded of a search I conducted for a $5.5B multinational company based in Chicago. This particular search was for a Human Resources Manager, to head HR at one of their manufacturing facilities in Cincinnati. One of the candidates I really liked and presented was an individual with a truly exceptional background. The candidate (we'll call him Barry) joined the USAF immediately after high school graduation, starting in the lowest enlisted rank. Fifteen years later he left the Air Force as a Captain and with a BS and MBA from an excellent university, also obtained while in the Air Force. Those of you with a military background know that this type of advancement in a peacetime military is in fact exceptional! An individual must have ability, intelligence, strong political skills and aggressiveness to own such a track record. After leaving the Air Force, Barry had gained six years of HR experience with a Japanese automotive manufacturing company in one of their U.S. operations. I met with him, was impressed, and arranged an interview with my client. After he met with my client, I received surprising feedback. They opted not to pursue him as a candidate. I was shocked, as I thought Barry would be a sure placement. When I asked the reason why, they indicated that though they thought he was very smart, had good HR experience and was likeable, they did not think that he would be aggressive enough to work in their environment. Because the last part of the feedback—lack of aggressiveness—was the antithesis of my assessment, I asked how they came to that conclusion. They indicated that because Barry did not make eye contact with the division President (who would have been his boss) during their interview, he gave the impression that he was not self-confident and lacked aggressiveness.

When I gave the feedback to Barry, he was naturally disappointed—but he had an answer for why the President may have gotten the impression that he was not aggressive and lacked self-confidence. He stated that because he had worked for a Japanese company for 6 years, he had adapted his personal style to succeed in that culture. Barry explained that in a Japanese company it is considered disrespectful to make eye contact when communicating with very senior management—hence, when he met with the President, he treated him as he would a Japanese senior executive and didn't make direct eye contact. Even though I called my client and explained the rationale of Barry's behavior, it was too late. The perception had already been formed and the damage done. I wound up completing the search with a different candidate, but I've always felt that Barry would have been the better choice.

The moral to this story is that eye contact is an important, non-verbal queue in our culture. I'm not suggesting you engage in a stare-down with your interview, only that you maintain regular eye contact. Rather than allow an interviewer to jump to erroneous conclusions regarding your sincerity, aggressiveness, etc., maintain regular eye contact with your interviewer. As the Barry story indicates, it makes a difference.

JUST LIKE GOLD, YOUR REFERENCES ARE A PRECIOUS COMMODITY

Many times, candidates provide references on their resumes or employment application, or are asked to provide references after a first interview, before a definite, mutual interest has been established. I do NOT recommend the release of any reference information until the interview process has moved to a point where solid mutual interest has been established. In fact, I personally advise my candidates not to release their references until such time as an offer is forthcoming. The reason is that your references are comparable to gold—a very precious commodity—not to be spent needlessly. My rationale is based on two facts:

1. The moment you release your references and they are contacted, someone else knows that you are seeking a new position. In any economy (but particularly in tough economies!) the fact that your search is known can be dangerous. On occasion, well-meaning references will bring others into your little secret in the interest of "saving" you for your current company. They may feel by letting your boss know you're looking, something can be done to retain you with the company in your current role. Others, not so well-meaning may spread the word through idle gossip. The end result can be the same, an untimely release of your references can put you into serious difficulty with your current company—as in your boss calling you into his office and commenting, "I understand that you been out interviewing with ABC company . . .". If your company is already in a downsizing mode, then you've just nominated yourself to sit in the ejection seat. The same is true if you have a promotion or salary increase pending—they could disappear because the

company, assuming you're going to leave anyway, decides to save its generosity for some other more deserving and loyal soul.

Yes, there are exceptions to this "rule". On a few occasions, I have seen the exact opposite occur when the word got out that an individual was in the hunt. I have seen companies, as a pre-emptive strike, increase the pay or promote individuals when they got wind that the employee was actively interviewing. However, these exceptions aside, in the vast majority of cases, the outcome of a premature disclosure of your search is likely to be negative. Releasing references before their proper time in the interview process is a high-risk behavior and can contribute to your being "outed" at your current company.

2. References tend to decrease in quality with use. What this means is that the more often your references are called, the lower the overall quality of the reference provided. In most cases, you will only provide references of people you trust to give you a good review. These are people who want to help you. However, even the most supportive ally will grow less eager when they've been

contacted 2, 3, 4, 5, 6 or more times. Properly done, a reference should take 30-40 minutes. After your reference has been contacted several times and spent a few hours in total talking about you, they can begin to feel somewhat "put upon"; as in, "Can't this guy find a job?" Remember, people everywhere value their time and can find any number of reasons not to have it wasted. My point is that after the first four or five calls, even the most tolerant of people will begin to wish that you had nominated someone else to speak to prospective employers.

My advice: release your references only when an offer is imminent (and you feel that you'll accept) or when the company absolutely insists that they be provided to continue the process. Then it is time to use that request as a status check—to verify that the company does indeed have a serious interest in you as a candidate, and that you have a serious interest in the company. To release your references freely and without this consideration is to be done at your own peril.

TAKING NOTES DURING THE INTERVIEW

As I indicated earlier, I always encourage my candidates to take notes during their interviews. In school, the best students take thorough notes while in class to help them study for the test. Taking notes is important because:

First: Human memory can be very selective. The dynamic nature of interviews can cause you to forget important data or observations—denying you their use at decision time. Without taking notes, you may be forced to rely upon your "feelings" or the perceptions you have formed, neither of which may be based on fact. Relying on either, may cause you to make a less than informed decision with regard to accepting or rejecting an offer.

Second: We are going to use the notes that you take to help us "close the circle"—even after the interview—when you write your "Thank You" letter to the interviewer. To be able to do this, you'll need to pay particular attention to the questions asked you by the interviewer. When your background was discussed, was there anything for which interviewer showed particular interest or enthusiasm? Were there areas where you felt your background totally matched the specification? Were there any apparent "holes" in your background (i.e. areas in which you were lacking the right experience) when comparing it to the job requirements? What were the challenges presented by the position as defined by the interviewer? What are the major projects or assignments of significance that are on-going or upcoming? Also, record any "personal anecdotes" (such as vacations taken or planned by the interviewer, "war stories" shared, memorable events from the interview, etc.) that might have arisen from the meeting. Again, in a later section, we'll discuss how you will be using some or all of this data when you write your high-impact "Thank You" letter.

Third: Another important reason for taking notes is that during the interview you are continually creating perceptions for your interviewers to assess. A candidate who takes notes during the interview can't help but appear to be a serious and thoughtful candidate in the mind of the interviewer. The reality is that most interviewers will assume that this sterling quality will continue even after you've become an employee—not a bad perception to create!

Fourth: When you take notes during your interview, there is another, more subtle perception you're creating. You are, in effect, paying a large compliment to your interviewer—because by your actions you are indicating that what they are saying is <u>noteworthy</u>! Suffice to say, the perception that their words are worthy of someone taking note, is going to make your interviewer feel good about himself—which is another opportunity to build rapport with your interviewer.

ASKING QUESTIONS (BEFORE) AND DURING THE INTERVIEW

I've always thought that the very best candidates are not just those people who give the greatest answers, but those who ask the best questions. Candidates who ask probing and meaningful questions demonstrate their intellectual horsepower, inquisitiveness and a desire to "get it right"—meaning, to gather enough data upon which to make a good and lasting decision regarding their careers long term. Correspondingly, I always challenge my clients prior to starting a search to demonstrate their understanding of the role for which they'd like me to recruit. This is critical—as not only does it prevent your favorite recruiter from wasting his time chasing a constantly-moving target—it also helps to assure that the hiring company has come to agreement as to the nature of the role, its true responsibilities, the "deliverables" they expect the incumbent to produce—and over how long a period of time. Having this understanding and commitment agreed to in advance is important—as I want all of my candidates to achieve success in their new roles. After all, it's good for business!

I know you wouldn't be surprised to read that many people are hired without their bosses being totally sure about what they want the newly-hired individual to accomplish—or that people are hired with resources inadequate to accomplish their mission. The net result in these cases is usually job failure—with the individual "on the hook" for having failed to deliver. My primary issue with this type of job failure is that the outcome was so easily preventable—simply by asking the right questions up front. However, to prevent this type of job failure, both the hiring manager/s AND the candidate need to truly consider the scope, responsibilities, freedom to act, and resources required for the role to be considered successful and ask the salient questions – BEFORE an offer is extended and accepted. To that end, here are just a few of the questions that I'd recommend that you ask and are able to answer BEFORE accepting any job offer:

1. In a short paragraph, describe the company—its products/services, overall mission, operating geography, size, and plans for the future.

2. In no more than 3 sentences describe the overall responsibilities for this role.

3. List as many day-to-day or regular "responsibilities" that you would expect to be accountable for delivering (e.g. a "task list") during your first 12 months.

4. Where would you like to be positioned at 30 days, 60 days, and 120 days relative to your progress in this role?

5. At the end of 12 months, how will your success or failure be determined, e.g. upon which criteria? You could consider this to be your performance appraisal "in advance".

6. What are 3 unique "deliverables" for which you'd expect to be held accountable for

completing during your first 12 months? Projects or assignments should be specific and with timelines. N.B. These are in addition to the "normal" responsibilities identified in #3?

7. What are the challenges, or barriers to success, you'd expect to face during your first year with the company?

8. What resources exist presently to help you accomplish your mission?

9. What resources will have to be added or obtained to help the you accomplish your mission?

10. How able is the company to adequately fund the acquisition of the resources identified in #9?

Get these questions answered during your interview and you'll have lots of good data upon which to make a lasting decision!

A QUICK DIVERSION—A GREAT WEBSITE FOR JOB SEEKERS

Before we move forward, I'd like to take a quick diversion into the web-based, job posting arena. As I indicated at the outset, my intent in writing this book has always been to be more strategic in nature vs. tactical. Put in a different manner, my goal has been to give you a sense of how to <u>think</u>, not what to <u>do</u>. There are just too many variables in the recruiting process for one book to cover every contingency. I've always felt that if you understand the underlying strategy covering an event, then you can create the correct tactics to best handle any specific circumstance. So, even though this is not a book on tactics, per se, there is a website that I've bumped into, that is just so good, I have to share it.

I'm sure that virtually every reader of this book has used web-based recruiting sites such as Monster.com, CareerBuilder, Dice, etc. in their job search. Companies pay Monster, et al, a fee to post their available positions—that fee being approximately $250-$450 per posting. As you can imagine, because of the cost involved, a company will not post all of its positions on these fee-based outlets (e.g.

Monster.com).   However, if that company has a corporate website, most likely, on that website will be a "Careers" link/page. This section will list many, but not all, (e.g. senior-level management or executive positions are usually not posted) of the positions for which the company is currently recruiting.   With unlimited time, you could search every corporate website and personally sift through the thousands of jobs that are available (the operative word being "unlimited") to find positions for which to apply. The downside is that the time required to perform such a thorough search of all companies—and for a specific type of position meeting your qualifications—would be prohibitive.   Is there an alternative to this time-consuming, but important means of ferreting out as many job openings as possible?

Yes! That alternative is a website called, "LinkUp.com" (www.linkup.com). LinkUp functions as a job posting aggregator—in other words, LinkUp is a search engine that searches only corporate web pages (i.e. the "Careers" section of a corporate website) and assembles the relevant job postings based on the search criteria entered. The site is very easy to use, very fast and generates targeted results (by company name, city/zip code, job title, company size, etc.). It's a great site for job seekers and I highly recommend it as another tool in your job search toolkit.

Okay, we have completed the Pre-Interview preparation phase of the process (my singular attempt at alliteration!) and are now ready to discuss the main event, the interview itself. I am certain that by now, many of you who are reading this are thinking, "Does he really expect me to do all of these things before an interview? This is real work!" The answer to your unspoken question is "Yes", I do! As I stated before, your interview is a performance—and the quality of any performance is dictated by the amount of preparation and rehearsal beforehand.

SECTION IV -- THE INTERVIEW

THE INTERVIEW

When I teach my graduate classes or give corporate seminars, I always ask the participants a basic question—what is an interview? At the core of this simple question is the rationale behind everything we do and every perception we create — so that we can succeed in the recruiting process and receive a job offer.

Let's start by stating what an interview is not! An interview is <u>not</u> an interrogation. An interview is <u>not</u> a time for you to sit back and have "your buttons pushed" and be in response mode to the interviewer's questions. It is <u>not</u> a venue for a company to assume that your life will only be complete if you come to work for them, on their terms and subject to their whims.

Stated directly, an interview, at its best, is a two-way conversation—**a dialogue between two equals**. This is why I so adamantly stress the importance of candidates having thoroughly researched the firm, being well prepared for the meeting and creating the right perceptions in the mind of their interviewer(s). To achieve true "dialogue", several factors must take place. First, you must convey the image that you are meeting with the company as an equal—that is, there is an equal benefit to be gained by both parties if you join forces. Second, you must use the interview to determine whether the prospective company has a culture and environment that is compatible with your style and personal Success Matrix. Third, you must be well prepared for the interview—being so, will create a feeling of self-confidence and help to put you at ease. Fourth, one of your goals should be to create an image that speaks to your potential for success in the company. As I stated at the very beginning of our discussion, it is not always the "best" candidate that receives an offer—it is the best prepared, qualified candidate who prevails.

TYPES OF INTERVIEWS

Although the terminology has changed in the past few years, there are two primary styles of interviews. They are: the Functional Interview and the Behavioral Interview.

FUNCTIONAL VS. BEHAVIORAL INTERVIEWS: WHICH ONE ANSWERS THE "CAN" VS. "WILL" QUESTION?

As its name implies, a functional interview centers on a candidate's ability to perform a specific job *function*. For example, if you are a programmer, to what extent do you know C++, PHP, or JAVA? If you are interviewing for a Sales Representative position, are the products or services you have sold and your industry's sales cycle similar to the interviewing company's? Did you make quota? Can you understand the technology of the product you'll be selling, etc.? For a CFO role, what experience have you had with derivatives, swaps, or foreign currency exchange? How strong is your network in the financial community? Have you successfully led a large financial organization, etc.?

In simple terms, *functional interviews* "test" whether you as the candidate "CAN" do the job. That is, do you have the necessary technical competence and proficiency to execute the responsibilities of the position in an acceptable fashion?

By contrast, the *behavioral interview* seeks to answer the all-important question of: "WILL" you do the job; that is "can vs. will". In other words, does your past history suggest that you possess the "behaviors" and "competencies" required to perform at a high level and can you replicate those behaviors and perform at a similar level in the environment and culture of the new company? Behavioral interviews also assess what your potential might be within the firm—e.g. are you promotable to more senior positions in the company?

First-tier companies go to great effort and expense to define their "core competencies"; that is, the qualities and attributes necessary to achieve success in their culture. This process involves both identifying the success traits of high-performing individuals within the firm, and also attempting to understand the traits or qualities that have caused people to fail. For the company, the output of this exercise is a *Competency Model*, or a set of characteristics that define success in the company. After this model is developed, interview questions are formulated to "test" the level to which a candidate matches up against each competency. Often, different interviewers are assigned to "test" different competencies.

On the following pages, is an example of a "Competency Model" used by a hypothetical corporation and the corresponding "Candidate Evaluation Form" based on the that Competency Model. The competencies listed are those that have been identified as being necessary to achieve success within our hypothetical company. Note that the Candidate Evaluation Form not only asks for a numerical rating (1-4), but also requires that the interviewer list specific behaviors (past examples of your performance) that support their rating. Once you get a handle on the methodology behind behavioral interviewing (i.e. interviewers are looking for specific behaviors to support their "findings"), you'll understand why I stress answering questions in the manner I do. Your goal is to make certain that you never allow an interviewer to <u>assume</u> anything about you or your background; that is, to "guess" what you've done. We want to give them enough specific data, so that they have no choice but to make a "call" on us based on the real, positive aspects of our background versus the imagined or assumed. Remember our discussion earlier about "claim" statements. It is important that our statements be regarded as factual, not simply claims which can be either quickly dismissed or worse, be open to interpretation. We'll discuss this in detail, when

I explain the difference between a "claim" statement and a "fact" statement in a later section.

ABC CORPORATION
COMPETENCY MODEL

1. **Intellectual Ability**—The ability to think logically and conceptually; the ability to use innovative thought and envision new ideas.

2. **Decisiveness**—The ability to "take a stand" on issues; the ability to make a clear choice in the face of alternatives; demonstrated self-confidence in abilities.

3. **Energy/Enthusiasm**—The capacity to work vigorously and actively without fatigue; the ability to express positive attitudes and emotions; possessing a sense of humor in difficult situations.

4. **Results Orientation**—The desire and commitment to achieve practical results.

5. **Team Orientation**—The ability to be "non-territorial"; the ability to work with others cooperatively and share responsibilities and rewards.

6. **Openness**—The ability to admit to mistakes and take criticism; possessing a sense of self-awareness of impact on others; capacity to express ideas freely.

7. **Initiative**—The ability to work towards project completion without close supervision; willingness to challenge the "status quo" and accept a moderate degree of risk.

8. **Flexibility**—Willingness to accept and prosper in the face of ambiguity and changing priorities; desire to confront and embrace new ideas.

ABC CORPORATON
COMPETENCY MODEL
CANDIDATE EVALUATION FORM

Candidate Name: _____

COMPETENCY	SPECIFIC BEHAVIORS TO SUPPORT RATING	RATING (1=OUTSTANDING)
Intellectual Ability		1 2 3 4
Decisiveness		1 2 3 4
Energy/ Enthusiasm		1 2 3 4
Results Orientation		1 2 3 4
Team Orientation		1 2 3 4
Openness		1 2 3 4
Initiative		1 2 3 4
Flexibility		1 2 3 4

Refer/Hire? ☐ Yes ☐ No   Interviewer: _____

Comments: _____
_____
_____
_____

THE FOUR MAJOR PHASES IN EVERY EMPLOYMENT INTERVIEW

Every employment interview, whether functional, behavioral, 15-minute "Look-See", or 2-hour assessment, is comprised of the same elements, although they may be present in different proportions based on the individual style of the interviewer and the time available. The four elements are:

1. **Warm-up/Opening** – a good warm-up is crucial to the success of an interview. Remembering our psychology experiment earlier, we want to help our interviewer "close the circle". Be confident! Remember, you are sitting in that office because they <u>wanted</u> you to be there! Use the "warm-up" as a platform to move the interview towards success.

   The warm-up is the period where both parties are getting in sync with each other and creating a climate where questions can be asked and answered (dialogue, remember!). It also sets the tone for the future relationship between the parties. Many people feel that the warm-up should be reduced to talking about the "weather" or whether "you had any trouble finding the building", etc. When these become the topics of the warm-up, the parties miss a terrific opportunity to build real rapport with each other. My suggestion is to use non-controversial, but topical issues to discuss. For example, look around the interviewer's office to determine if there are areas of common ground. Do you see pictures of family or children? Are there tennis or golf trophies or other paraphernalia? These are all good conversation starters during the warm-up. For example:

I can remember a final interview I had with a company's Senior VP of Human Resources. Entering his office, I noticed a picture of William T. Sherman, a famous (Sherman's March to the Sea) and extremely effective Union General in the Civil War. I took a guess that the VP of HR was either a Civil War or military history buff (or both) and asked his opinion of whether he thought that Sherman should be considered "famous" or "notorious". He smiled and said, "I guess it depends on which side of the line you were." We then spent the next 5 minutes discussing

Civil War history and Sherman's later promotion to General-in-Chief of the Army under President Grant. During that period, we had a chance to get to know one another on a more personal basis. It made the rest of the interview a true dialogue and led to greater exchange of information.

2. **Their Agenda** – This phase is dedicated to responding to the questions of the interviewer. We will explore this section in depth, when we discuss THE FIVE QUESTIONS.

3. **Your Agenda** – Phase Three is your agenda. Remember, a great interview is a <u>dialogue</u>—an exchange of information between two parties. As we discussed in "Pre-Interview Preparation", make certain that you exercise this opportunity to ask the complex questions which you have prepared in advance.

4. **Conclusion and Housekeeping** – The concluding phase of the interview is what I call "housekeeping". In this phase you are able to ask questions not directly related to the job or company, but instead focus on the "next steps"

in the process. Don't be shy about asking the interviewer when a decision will be made regarding the position and about expressing your sincere interest in the company. This is also a good time to express confidence in the future of the company and how, specifically, you can make a contribution to the growth of the firm.

THE FINAL 3 MINUTES

The final 3 minutes of the interview is absolutely critical for you to observe and remember! It is during that period of time that interviewers will usually "tip their hand" as to what they thought of the interview and you. So, pay very close attention to what they say during this time, how they respond to your final questions and you! When I debrief my candidates, asking about the final 3 minutes of the interview is always among the top 3 questions I ask. I can usually put together a fairly accurate picture of "how the interview went" and the type of feedback I'll be getting from my client regarding the candidate.

As a final aside, based on how you felt the interview progressed you could ask the interviewer how you "match up" against the requirements of the position.

However, you will need to carefully consider the relationship and rapport you've established with your interviewer before you ask. Asking for a "call" can cause the interviewer to react defensively. Don't forget, you are putting your interviewer on the spot—and not everyone likes to be there. Not every candidate can pull this off, so I do NOT recommend this approach for everyone. But, those candidates who successfully execute this tactic, are invariably seen as assertive and confident, and as expressing their "true" interest in the role. These are all great things for which to be remembered as a candidate. Another benefit to this approach is that it's also like getting your performance appraisal on the spot. You'll have a very good idea of "where you stand."

If you choose this approach, take the feedback and do NOT argue the points—unless your interviewer has gotten something fundamentally wrong—and you can prove it with facts. Attempting to debate an opinion with your interviewer at this point most often will lead to disaster! Just think: you've just asked your interviewer for an opinion, they took a risk and gave it to you, and now you want to debate it point-by-point? In my opinion, that is definitely a losing call.

THE ART OF THE QUESTION

I'm going to focus this section on the types of questions skilled interviewers use. Please note that I am not going to provide you with a list of questions and their corresponding "stock" answers. There have been many books written that address typical interview questions and their "best answers". We've all read them. Unfortunately, though, so has our interviewer. To the interviewer, responding in "stock" fashion will make you sound canned and artificial and lacking credibility—not the image you want to project. Plus, "stock" answers may not express your actual feelings or thoughts on an issue. Please note that while I counsel honesty when answering questions (you'll never get in trouble telling the truth), being honest does not mean that we go out of our way to tell the interviewer how awful we are. What "being honest" does mean is that we don't invent or fabricate our responses. Also, avoid the temptation to over-commit when answering questions. Remember, you'll have to deliver on anything you said as a candidate once you become an employee!

So, instead of discussing specifically <u>what</u> to say, we're going to discuss the <u>types</u> of questions that skilled interviews utilize and <u>how</u> we should formulate our answers to those types of questions.

OPEN VS. CLOSED-ENDED QUESTIONS

The best interviewers make extensive use of *Open-Ended* questions. Open-Ended questions require you to explain not only what you did, but <u>why</u> you did it. An example: "Why did you choose to join XYZ Corporation knowing they were facing a potential Chapter 11?" Open-Ended questions generate a significant amount of data and lend themselves nicely to follow-ups and probes (more on these later).

Closed-Ended questions generally elicit a fact response or "yes/no" answer. For example, "Did you leave your last position because you were interested in a higher salary?" is a Closed-Ended question. As an aside, to make the question open-ended and increase the amount of data/behaviors generated by the candidate, the interviewer should ask the same question like this: "How important a factor was compensation in your decision to leave XYZ Corporation?" You can see how your response to the same question would be markedly different. You have to "give up" much more information about your values, choices, etc. when answering the Open-Ended variety.

Open-Ended questions generally stick to the "W$_5$H formula" (<u>W</u>ho, <u>W</u>hat, <u>W</u>hy, <u>W</u>here, <u>W</u>hen, and <u>H</u>ow). Listen to the words used at the beginning of the question to determine if your interviewer is following the W$_5$H formula. Examples: <u>Who</u> are the people who have most influenced your professional career? <u>What</u> was most important to you about that project? <u>Why</u> did you leave your last company? <u>Where</u> do you see yourself in 5 years? <u>When</u> do you feel that you'll be ready for your next move? <u>How</u> did you make that choice?

Incidentally, Closed-Ended questions are often used by interviewers to stop "filibusters"—that is, when candidates are consuming valuable interview time with rambling or non-responsive answers. If you find yourself in the middle of the interview suddenly being asked a series of Closed-Ended questions where before the interviewer had been using primarily Open-Ended questions, think about the responses you gave earlier in the meeting. If on reflection, you would have to admit that you were rambling, then you know the reason for the shift in the type of question being asked. More important, you just got an opportunity to "fix" the problem and recover before the end of the interview by becoming more direct and responsive—hopefully, before permanent damage has been done (as in, "I couldn't get a straight answer out of him", or "He was all over the map with his answers", or "He had no focus.").

FORCED-CHOICE QUESTIONS

Forced-Choice questions are used by the most skilled interviewers when they want to pin candidates down— very often into picking between the lesser of two evils. Mike Wallace of *60 Minutes* fame and the Sam Donaldson (formerly of ABC's *This Week*), were the masters of the Forced-Choice question. Lawyers and police interrogators also love this type of question. For example, you might be asked by an interviewer, "So was the reason you left XYZ Corporation because of difficulties with your boss or with your co-workers?" When you think about the choices you have in answering this question, either choice is a bad one. If you say "co-workers", then you are portrayed as someone who's not a team player. If you answer, "My boss", then you're painted as someone who can't take direction and has a difficult time working for others. In most cases, a skilled interviewer will not be as obvious in the choices they give you (in this case, both were clearly negative), but will instead give you subtler choices designed to probe if you're going to be a good fit within their culture or for a particular job. For example, you could be asked, "So it sounds as though you prefer managing a team versus contributing directly as an individual." On the surface this might seem a harmless enough question. But, just suppose the role for which you're interviewing, Director of Marketing, requires you to spend at least half your time as an individual contributor and the other half of your time managing a team. You might be fooled by the job's title into thinking that managing the team is where the company is focusing, so you respond, "Yes, I get my greatest satisfaction in building a team and leading it towards project completion." The next thing you know, you've been rejected as a candidate. Your recruiter later tells you that the company heard you state that *you didn't like being an individual contributor.* And, here's the "assume" word at work—because at least half of the job required you to be an individual contributor, they *assumed* that you "wouldn't be happy in the role". Too late at this point to disagree—you've just been done in by a Forced-Choice question. N.B., to demonstrate the power of the word "assume", just remember how it's spelled—it can make an "ass" out of "u" and "me".

COMPARISON AND CONTRAST QUESTIONS

My own personal favorite is the Comparison and Contrast question. These are very powerful questions because they force a candidate to think about the choices they've made and why they've made them. In behavioral interviewing, they are great for generating behaviors and values, which can give the interviewer terrific insight into a candidate's future behaviors. An example of a Comparison and Contrast question is: "How would you compare the culture of Deloitte Consulting to that of Accenture?" And of course, the follow-up, "In which company did you feel the more comfortable?" As you can see, this type of question, properly asked and probed, generates significant data regarding values, choices, and how an individual makes decisions.

PROBES

Probes are follow-ups to questions already asked. There are many, but I'll discuss two. First, there is what I call, the "How/Why so?" probe. For example, you might answer a question, "It was really important to me to become a manager at XYZ Corporation." Your interviewer probes with, "You mentioned that it was important that you became a manager at XYZ. Why so?" Or, you might answer a question, "We really made an impact on the company completing that project." To probe, an interviewer will ask, "Really—how so?"

A second type of probe, used by the most skilled interviewers, is the calculated "Pregnant Pause". As an example, have you ever been asked a question, given your answer, only to get no reaction from the interviewer, but silence? You know that the interviewer is seeking more information, but instead of asking a follow-up question, they just continue to silently look at you. Seconds pass that seem like hours. Finally, you succumb to the pressure and blurt something out—anything, just to relieve the abominable pressure!

The interviewer gains a great advantage when using this technique. Most candidates when asked an interview question already have a response prepared mentally, which they give. However, when faced with a "Pregnant Pause", candidates feel the overwhelming need to "fill the gap" (which seems like an eternity!) with additional information—usually without having had a chance to think the additional response through and put the filters on. Hence, the additional information given is likely to be a much more revealing statement of a candidate's true feelings on an issue then was the initial response. The answer "blurted out" in response to a Pregnant Pause can very often be the answer that sinks a candidate's ship.

Your correct response to the Pregnant Pause is to wait just a few more seconds to determine if another question is forthcoming from the interviewer to probe your previous response. When you sense no further questions are in the offing, then just smile and ask, "Is this the type of information you were looking for?", or, "Did I respond to your question?", or "Were you looking for more information?" The proper tactic is to pass the baton back to your interviewer in the form of a question—placing the onus for "filling the gap" on him. At that point, he can either clarify his intent or move on to the next question. In either case, you haven't opened the door to potential disaster by "winging it" with an answer that you've not had sufficient time to mentally screen. Of course, you could just stare your interviewer down and "play chicken" with him, but to what end? We're here to win the game, not just play it!

RESPONDING TO QUESTIONS

Having discussed the many types of questions that are asked on interviews, one can see the importance of knowing how to respond most effectively. Fortunately, being a *pro* at answering questions is a skill that can be easily learned by applying a few simple guidelines.

As an example, most successful politicians must develop the skill of effectively answering questions—if they are to survive in a world in which everything they say is parsed and analyzed (as in, ". . . It depends on what the meaning of 'is' is."). The next time you watch one of the Sunday morning political programs, notice how the politician being asked the question performs. While the interviewer is asking the question, the politician doesn't comment, doesn't react or interrupt, and in most cases, doesn't even nod their head to indicate that they've understood the question. They only begin to answer the question when the interviewer comes to a complete stop—and if they're unsure of the question, they'll repeat it and get confirmation before they begin their response. The reason for this is that people who interrupt interviewers in mid-question, *assuming* they know what's being asked, are very often wrong about the intent of the question being asked, and/or give a non-responsive answer—or worse, commit themselves to a position without understanding the true nature of the question. My counsel is that before you answer a question, make very certain you know what is being asked. I am <u>not</u> suggesting you participate in the double-talk and non-answers that politicians give—that would be damaging to your case. I <u>am</u> suggesting that you not respond to a question until you understand what is being asked—clarify if you need to, but wait until the question has been fully asked.

The manner in which you respond to questions is also key to creating the right perceptions about your candidacy. I say this because I have spoken with many candidates over the years who have placed their own value judgments on the questions being asked and have responded accordingly. For example, after an interview I'll get feedback from a candidate such as, "It wasn't a fair question to ask." or "His questions made no sense. They had nothing to do with the job. Why would I want to give him a good answer?"

This lack of considered response can be damaging to a candidate's chances. Despite the fact that we might not understand the rationale behind the interviewer's question, the interviewer usually <u>does</u> have a reason for asking it. For example, an interviewer could ask, "If you could change anything about yourself, what would it be?" An applicant might think that the interviewer is probing for his weak points, when in reality the interviewer is looking for much more. He could be probing for the level of the candidate's maturity and self-awareness (measured by the depth of the response); he could be assessing a candidate's openness or their ability to deal with negative information (incidentally, this is an attribute of "Openness", one of the competencies in our sample Competency Matrix.). So, as it turns out, this "simple" question was actually much more complex.

Staying focused throughout the interview is also important when answering questions. Many candidates start the interview in fine shape—they're well prepared and rehearsed for the first round of questions. However, as the interview drags on, they are moved further away from their "comfort zone" and lose focus on what is being asked. I've received client feedback stating that they were prepared to hire a candidate in the first 20 minutes of the interview only to change their mind as the final 20 minutes degenerated into unfocused and non-responsive answers to questions. Needless to say, those candidates did not receive offers!

BEEN WITH YOUR COMPANY FOR 5+ YEARS? BETTER READ THIS SECTION!

Okay, I'm probably going to upset a few people again, but I feel it would be irresponsible of me not to comment on the question answering capabilities of "long service" candidates. By "long service" candidates I am referring to those people who have spent 8+ years with their current company or have been away from the interview experience for 5+ years. In my experience, this type of candidate often learns very painful lessons from their first 2-3 interviews. Unfortunately, however, when this lesson is learned during the interview, the individual usually finds themselves rejected as a candidate. Learning to interview effectively by experience, that is, by failing on the first few interviews and then using those lessons to improve your performance (or in other words, trial and error!) can be problematic in a tight job market. You might only get two or three good (i.e. for positions in which you truly have an interest) interviews in 6 months! Even in a good job market, you don't want to blow a great opportunity because you weren't prepared.

To be direct, "long-service" candidates typically have a difficult time answering direct questions, directly. That is, they tend to give long, rambling monologues that are non-responsive to simple questions; or, fill their answers with company-related jargon, and names and anecdotes that are certain to be lost on their interviewers who come from a different environment. Long-service candidates may also lack the "hire-me" energy or "polish" that a more frequently engaged candidate has. All of these issues are symptomatic of only a lack of practice and interviewing experience. For example:

A candidate I interviewed recently was the VP Human Resources with an $1B+ financial services company. He had been with his company for 15 years—beginning his career as an HR Representative; and through subsequent promotions, he had assumed the top HR role in his firm. He was an intelligent, articulate and highly competent HR professional. However, he had not been on an interview in over 10 years. To say the least, he was out of practice.

Wanting to test his ability to respond quickly after having been out of the game for 10+ years, I asked him to "take me briefly through your background." I was looking for a 2-3 minute response—an overview of his background (more about this later when we discuss "The 5 Questions"). What I received was a rambling, chronological, 10-minute "core dump" of his entire work history (he would have spoken longer if I had allowed him to continue) that overwhelmed me with data—both important and trivial. As mentioned, I was expecting him to be out of practice given the time since his last interview. My mission was to determine where we needed to spend time prior to his upcoming interview so that he could more effectively articulate his background. Mission accomplished on this one!

In response to further questions, he gave similar long, jargon-filled, non-responsive answers. He was committing the cardinal interviewing "sin"; that is; giving too much information! He was working too hard trying to anticipate what I was seeking in the way of information and felt it was best to give me too much rather than not enough—which is analogous to shooting an ant with a shotgun. In an actual interview setting, he would have been perceived as non-responsive and rambling—which would have been an erroneous perception as he was anything but.

Why does this happen? Why do otherwise intelligent and demonstrably successful people "lose it" on an interview?

Consider the profile of an individual who has had a long career with a single company. Over the years he has been successful. He has established credibility. His peers give him "license" to talk and even ramble on occasion because they are co-workers. Think about it . . . would you cut off an important colleague in mid-filibuster? You probably would not, as it wouldn't be politically smart to offend him. In other words, candidates coming from long-service backgrounds can pick up very bad habits in question answering. You get a great degree of latitude (from co-workers) when responding to questions in your workplace. The bad news is that your interviewer will cut you little or no slack. The time allocated for an interview is short and the interviewer is on a mission. A high-impact candidate helps their interviewer accomplish his mission.

The converse of rambling can also be true from long-service candidates. Often long-service candidates will fill their interviews with short, jargon-filled responses. Were they answering a fellow employee of their firm this would great, as this "jargon speak" is analogous to the "verbal shorthand" that every company has. For example, when I interview candidates from a former Big 5 accounting firm, I can be certain that I'll experience an interview loaded with abbreviations, acronyms, partner's names, etc.—all of which would be meaningful to a fellow employee, but mean little to me as a member of the uninitiated. Perfectly great experiences and anecdotes lose their impact because the interviewer does not understand the candidate's verbal shorthand. This verbal shorthand is distracting and meaningless to the non-initiated and can lead to the confounding of the interviewer. And, the last state we want our interviewer to be in . . . is in the state of confusion.

So, the message to those of you who are participating in your first interview in a number of years is: Don't assume that the rules that govern an interview are similar to those that govern your everyday business interactions within your company. The interaction within your company is analogous to a 1,000-meter run. The scenario that you'll be faced with in an interview is closer to a 100-meter dash. So, how do we overcome this tendency to run the wrong race? Very simply, we practice, practice, practice!

Interviewing is like any other acquired skill; e.g. typing, riding a bicycle, golf, etc. You have to practice to be great! Personally, I would rather you practice before the interview and use all of the resources available to you to test your readiness to sit in the hot seat. Participate in practice interviews and/or have your answers to specific questions videotaped and critiqued—most outplacement firms offer this service. You'll find it an illuminating experience to actually have a chance to see yourself on tape and get a sense for how you impact other people with your answers. If you do not have the services of an outplacement firm, use your own video camera, phone, iPad, etc. Observe and critique your own performance. Use colleagues, friends, spouses, etc. Have them listen to your responses to questions (particularly "The 5 Questions") and then provide you with their feedback. Are your answers focused and on-topic? Are they understandable and responsive? Are they given within the appropriate time parameters?

RESPONDING TO THE "MONEY" QUESTION

Speaking to the point of how being responsive to the interviewer's questions is extremely important, many candidates think that they can play dodge ball with certain questions. A prime case in point is the "Money Question"—as in, "What are you currently earning" or "What type of compensation are you looking for to make a move?" I feel strongly, after 30+ years of recruiting experience on both the corporate and search sides of the equation, that you must ultimately answer the "money" question. I know there are those who will strongly advise against giving a direct response to this question and that my position is open to debate. But, whoever these experts may be, I can state that one such hearty soul advising candidates not to answer this question cost me a placement several years ago! More about this in just a bit.

Candidates sometimes feel that in giving their salary information, they are giving up valuable leverage in the salary negotiations game. Let's say for example, we have a candidate who has 5 years of experience and is making $70K per year. They are interviewing for a job that requires 5-9 years of experience and will pay in the range of $75-95K annually. The recruiter has already told them the range, so the candidate goes into the interview thinking that a company is going to bring them from $70K to $95K—the top of the hiring range—representing a 35.7% increase! Unfortunately, they forget to factor into their thought process, that the $95K upper limit is there to accommodate candidates who possess 8-9 years of experience and who fully meet the job specification. So, what happens? When they are asked on the interview as to how much they are currently earning, they respond with, "I'd prefer not to discuss money at this point. I'd like to first find out more about the opportunity." or, "I'd be happy to discuss my salary expectations (not actual salary, you notice!) at a later time when we're closer to making a decision on whether I'm a good candidate." Or, "What I'm currently making is not important. I'd prefer to discuss what I'm worth to your organization based on my experience." In all three of these responses, the candidate is not answering a very important question. They think if they tell the interviewer that they're earning $70K, then the offer will be based on an increase over their current $70K salary rather than what they're "really" worth. In their mind, $95K is the correct answer!

It is true that companies use a candidate's current base salary as a reference point when formulating offers. However, companies have to be sensitive to market pressures, too. If they "lowball" an offer, they will probably end up losing the candidate to another firm sooner or later. Also, bear in mind that companies are not in the habit of giving 35.7% increases either! They have to take into consideration not only external competitiveness, but also, internal salary equity. You can be certain that at $95K, our 5-year candidate would be making more than the company's existing 5-year employees—creating internal salary inequity. The ultimate reality is that this same candidate would be highly incensed if his own company offered a 35.7% increase to a new hire. He would feel that he wasn't valued, that he was underpaid and being taken advantage of. Yes, he would be quite upset! Yet, he thinks he can finesse a new company into doing so for him. The simple fact is that most large companies tend to be very competitive and will have similar salary ranges for the same type of job. Corporations spend large dollars to fund compensation departments whose job it is to assure external competitiveness and internal equity. As a result, it's just not likely that an individual will be so dramatically underpaid in their current firm that the new company will be in a position to offer them a whopping increase to make a move. And if they do, that should raise another question . . . why?

Again, I know that some of you reading this will disagree with my stance that salary information should be given freely to the interviewing firm. I know that there are many "experts" who disagree. In fact, I admit there is an exception to this practice of disclosing salary data that we'll discuss later in this section. However, my experience is that disclosure is a better course to take than evasion. As a proof statement let me ask, would you buy anything of significance (e.g. house, car, etc.) without knowing the cost first? Aren't potential employers also consumers or buyers? Do you think they'd make a major purchase (hiring you) without first knowing the cost?

To illustrate this point, let me offer you a real event that took place about three years ago:

> I was recruiting for a client who I had worked with for 12 years as he moved between 3 different companies. I had recruited for him long enough to anticipate the questions he would ask and his reaction to most of the answers he would get to his questions. Ross (not his name, but close!), a VP of

Human Resources at a large, high-tech firm in Chicago, was a very open and ethical individual and a successful leader. He believed that one of the keys to his success in leading people was his ability to build trust through his openness.

Ross asked me to start a search for a Manager of Human Resources. He was prepared to pay up to a $90K base salary, plus a 25% bonus and stock options. The total package would come in around $110K, plus options. He stated he would like to have a candidate with up to 9 years of HR experience, but with a bit of maneuvering on his current team could hire a more junior person of about 4 years, if they were exceptional.

I interviewed a candidate on the phone with 5 years of experience. She had a reasonably good educational package (BA from excellent private school, MBA from a 3rd tier university) and great experience for a 5-year person—although her experience was entirely with a small company where she was a 1-person HR department. Based on our very positive phone conversation I referred her to Ross, with the caveat that we hadn't met in person. After reviewing her resume and listening to my reaction to her, Ross indicated that he wanted to meet with her and agreed to hold until the candidate and I could meet in person the following Monday. We set the interview for Tuesday at 9:00 AM. As he was going to be taking a long-weekend and would not be back until Tuesday, the timing was perfect. When I met the candidate the following Monday, everything went well—until I asked her salary. She would not tell me, despite 3 attempts at uncovering the answer. I was guessing that she was making about $45K and that she was afraid that if she told me her true salary, that either she would be seen as too light for the role, or would receive a low salary offer based on her current $45K salary. Unfortunately, she was already aware of the upper salary limit on the search. She had been referred to me by a more experienced candidate I had initially contacted, but who was not interested—that person had passed along the salary range to her. Despite my warnings that Ross would ask the question and expect a response, she stated, "What I'm making now is irrelevant. I expect to be paid what the job is worth!" Normally, that would be the end of our conversation, but as I indicated, Ross was already expecting to see her the next morning at 9:00 AM.

She met with Ross the next morning and I think you already know the ending to this story. Ross' feedback was that although she was on the "light side" of what he was looking for, he thought that she was a great candidate—smart, solid experience and great potential to grow into the job. He said, "Because I thought she was great, I was ready to hire her until . . ."

I broke in and said, "Let me tell you . . . until you asked her what she was earning, right?" Ross stated, "Correct! She wouldn't tell me! I explained to her I would be fair to her in any offer that I made, but that I needed to have at least an idea of what she was earning and what she was expecting in an offer. She still wouldn't tell me . . ."

Ross then indicated that despite the fact that she was a great candidate, he would not extend an offer, because of her unwillingness to open up to him on the salary issue. To Ross, this demonstrated that building trust with her would be difficult. Netting it out, her unwillingness to answer the salary question cost her a great opportunity.

When I called her with feedback, she was disappointed, but defiant! Without wanting to be an "I told you so", I asked her where she had gotten the advice not to reveal her salary. She finally told me a friend of hers, who had lost her job and was in outplacement, had been told by the outplacement firm in a training class, never to divulge salary information on an interview. Her friend had been told that doing so would weaken her position during salary negotiations and would result in a lower offer than if she asked to be paid "what the job is worth". However, with Ross, clearly that "strategy" backfired. She lost out on a great opportunity due to bad advice given by a friend—who if they follow their own advice, is going to be out of work for a long time and for the same reason.

As a footnote, this same candidate contacted me 2 months later, still looking. She immediately (without any prompting) volunteered to me that she had just received a salary increase to $47.8K!

The moral of our story is: answer the money question directly and without fanfare! Avoiding or attempting to finesse this question will provide you with little, if any, gain—and as the story indicates, could potentially cause you to lose out on a great opportunity. The time to begin "leveraging" an offer is after both parties have developed a mutual, definitive interest. We'll return to this topic in a later section, "Decision Time".

Now, how about the scenario where an interviewer asks you what you would *like* to earn? How should that question best be handled? My counsel is to give your interviewer a "range", versus a specific number. Giving a range versus pinning yourself down to a specific dollar amount, is an acceptable answer and is considered responsive. For example, let's suppose that you're earning a $180K base salary, plus bonus, and you know the job you're interviewing for will pay $190-210K base, plus bonus. Further, you know that in the current market, companies have been offering 8-10% increases to move. A great response in this scenario would be, "I'm seeking a base salary offer in the range of the $200's. By using a range, you increase the odds of giving the "right" answer. That is, you won't talk yourself out of a job by being $1,000 over the maximum of the hiring range or leave money on the table that would have been yours! More often than not, you, as a candidate, will not know the true extent that a company can "stretch" on a salary offer. If you give an exact dollar amount, say $195K, you might talk yourself out of $10K they would have offered had you used a range, as in "the $200's". Again, using ranges is a perfectly acceptable response to the "What are you looking for in the way of compensation" question.

I promised to discuss an exception to the need to answer the "money question", and here it is:

If you possess a high-demand talent or skill (that is both unique and very difficult to obtain) or are a very senior executive (e.g. CEO) and know that you are the definitive candidate for the search, then you will be given more latitude in the manner in which you answer this question. In this scenario you have the ultimate negotiating position and are holding most, if not all, of the cards in your hands. You can be a bit more hard-edged about the information you release.

However, 99.9% of all candidates are not in this enviable position, so my feelings about answering the money question can be summarized by stating: When asked the "money question", answer the question!

THE 5 QUESTIONS

We are at the point in our discussion where it is time to move beyond the philosophical and into the realm of the practical. We will now consider the actual core of the interview—the questions that will be asked.

Like you, I have read numerous books enumerating all of the possible questions that are asked on employment interviews and the related "best" answers to each of them. In fact, I walked through our local Borders over the weekend and counted 18 books on interviewing and "question-answering". Could the Library of Alexandria have had more? Certainly, if you could read enough of these books and experience enough interviews, you would begin to gain a sense of the questions asked on an interview and their "best" responses. However, this is not a practical scenario as this would mean that you would have to be willing to "fail" several times on interviews until you could learn the correct manner of responding to not only basic questions, but also their variants. That would be unacceptable. Further, my experience is that when candidates respond to questions with a "book" response, they sound stilted and artificial. This is also unacceptable.

Just suppose, though, that I could provide you with a methodology to develop your own, natural answers to over 90% of the questions that you'll be asked on any employment interview—regardless of type (functional, behavioral, etc.). Would you like to hear about it?

I'm assuming a "yes", as you've already paid for the answer. Simply put, the answers to virtually every question asked on an employment interview can be distilled from the answers to only 5 basic questions. I call them *The 5 Questions*. In fact, if you can master the answers to "The 5 Questions", you will have the foundation to present yourself effectively on any employment interview. As we discussed at the outset, the "most" qualified candidate doesn't always receive an offer. Hiring decisions are a function of both qualifications *and* perceptions. However, by answering questions effectively on an interview, you gain the ability to form very positive perceptions about your candidacy.

What you ask, are these five all-encompassing questions? They are:

1. Tell me about yourself?
2. Why would you leave your current position? (Or) Why did you leave your previous position?

3. What type of position are you looking for?

4. What are your strong points/weak points?

5. Where do you see yourself in 5 years?

When I present these questions to my candidates to help prepare them for their interviews, I often get this response: "Wait a minute, these sound familiar, but they don't cover <u>all</u> of the questions I've been asked." Or, "I've been asked these questions before—I already know how to answer them." To the first response I state again that 90%+ of the questions asked in an interview are either these five or variants or extensions of them. In essence, *The 5 Questions* are the archetypes for all questions asked on an employment interview. With regard to whether you have already been asked these questions before, I say what is relevant is only how you will answer them on your <u>next</u> interview—and that is what this section is all about! My goal for you is to answer these questions (and every question asked) with high impact—so as to separate you from the pack of candidates that are sure to be in the contest with you. To do so you will have to have done your pre-interview homework and follow the methodology that I'll provide you. Your homework includes the exercises found in Section II, including the development of an action-oriented resume. Developing successful, winning answers to *The 5*

Questions will require you to draw upon every facet of your pre-interview preparation.

Please note, that for each of *The 5 Questions* I'll also give examples of variants or extensions. Just remember, though, regardless of the variant of the question asked, it's all the same question.

Another thought before we begin. As with every other skill in which you seek to become expert, you will need to practice delivering your answers to these questions several times <u>before</u> the interview. Only through practice will you gain the ability to stay focused, time-sensitive and sounding conversational (vs. stilted or unnatural). My counsel is to use a watch or clock to time yourself (according to the guidelines we'll discuss) while you practice your responses with either another person or by yourself, using a video camera.

Okay, let's get started!

THE 5 QUESTIONS

QUESTION #1: TELL ME ABOUT YOURSELF?

Or:

- Walk me through your background/resume.
- What can you tell me about your experience?
- I noticed that you have been out of school for 12 years. What have you been doing since then?
- Can you describe your experience?
- Tell me about how you came to work at XYZ, Inc. (your current company)?

Before we discuss the methodology for developing a high-impact answer to this question, it is worth a digression to discuss why this question is typically the first question asked by the majority of interviewers. This discussion will help to explain how interviewers think and in many cases, what drives their behaviors on the interview. So, why is "Tell me about yourself" so frequently the first question asked? There are four basic reasons:

1. **"Unprepared" Interviewer** – Let's describe the typical scenario leading to your interview and presence in the "hot seat".

You've submitted your resume to a company where it was screened—usually by the HR Representative. After passing "muster" with HR, your resume is then sent to the hiring manager who also reviews it. He does not review yours in a vacuum, but instead is most likely comparing it to 10-15 others that have been sent him. Bear in mind that this group of 10-15 resumes may have been chosen from literally hundreds of resumes— so the fact that you are still in the game is very good news! The hiring manager then provides the HR rep with the names of the people he wants to meet and asks HR to begin arranging interviews. Let's say, further, that he has chosen five candidates to interview and you're among them. So far, so good—you've made the "short list". To continue our example, let's also assume that he makes his decision and contacts HR on a Wednesday. HR then begins to contact the five chosen candidates to schedule meeting times. Because of the usual scheduling conflicts, interviews won't begin until the following Wednesday—7 days after the hiring manager has "green-lighted" your resume. You will be the first candidate scheduled to meet with the manager—your meeting is set for the following Wednesday at 9:00 AM.

As a practical matter, we've made a huge assumption in setting up our scenario. As anyone who has submitted a resume knows, 1-week turnaround is exceptionally quick. Often candidates can wait up to a month from the date they have submitted their resume to the time their interview date actually arrives. Getting back to our scenario . . .

You're now in the lobby and promptly at 9:00 AM the hiring manager meets you, shakes hands and off you go to his office. As you sit down, you notice that he has picked your resume up and has started to read it, as if for the first time, and then asks, "Tell me about yourself."

When considering this scenario, you are probably thinking that your interviewer has spent the past seven days carefully studying your resume, pondering your background and experience, and formalizing complex penetrating questions to ask during your meeting . . . right? Not right!

Even though he may have spent considerable time initially analyzing the backgrounds of the candidates he decided to interview, since that moment a week ago, much has happened. In that 7-day period he has had to resolve 2 serious production problems; he has had to terminate a non-performing employee; he has met with his boss and discussed a product line extension for the new model year; he has coached 2 soccer games; cleaned the garage, etc. I think you get the idea! The next thing he knows is that it is now 9:00 AM on Wednesday and the receptionist has just informed him that you're in the lobby ready for your meeting. He hurriedly takes your resume from his desk drawer (or brings it up on his computer monitor), looks at the name to make certain he remembers it, places the resume on his desk and quickly walks towards the lobby to pick you up.

After he gets you comfortably seated, he begins to scan your resume to re-familiarize himself with your background—mentally re-affirming his earlier decision to invite you in for an interview. His "Tell me about yourself" initial question allows him time to again read through your resume and get mentally re-connected with your background while you talk.

Bear in mind, I am not casting this hiring manager in a negative light. His schedule is no different than any other busy executive attempting to do their job and everything else in their life. Interviewing candidates is only one of those many things. As important as this manager feels meeting you is, like any other human being, he will place you as #1 priority only at 9:00 AM on the Wednesday of your interview. As an aside, his actions throughout the rest of the recruiting process will be a function of his priorities—be on the lookout for them. Understanding his priorities may help you better understand the pace of activity at which the search will proceed.

2. **The Interviewer May Himself be Nervous** – and getting you to talk first allows him time to relax and assume a position of leadership in the interview.

As someone who has been a candidate, I can tell you that I have felt nervousness before certain interviews, because as we discussed in a preceding section, all candidates feel some degree of tension prior to and even during an interview. Interestingly enough, in many cases the interviewer can be nervous at the outset of an interview, too! Remember, an employment interview is not a natural, every day event. For many hiring managers it is an activity that they perform only rarely. Also, just as a candidate seeks to be "liked", so does the hiring manager seek to create a positive impression so as to be "liked" by the candidate. Who knows, you may be running the entire company some day and he may be working for you! If you're as great a candidate as you appear on paper (after all, that's why he invited you in!), then he is going to want to be at his best so as to impress you enough to generate your interest in him, his job and the company—so he can hire you! Not the least of his tension can come from the fact that he knows that this hiring decision is critically important to his own career success. The sum of these concerns generates a fair amount of pressure on the hiring manager (and you thought only you were the only one under pressure!)—which can result in an initial level of nervousness. The "Tell me about yourself" question takes the onus temporarily off the interviewer and places it on the candidate— allowing the interviewer to relax a bit and gain control of the situation. This is actually a good thing—would you choose to be interviewed by a hiring manager who was not totally in control or nervous? In that scenario it is doubtful that a good decision could be made by either party.

3. **"Tell me about yourself" is non-confrontational and allows both parties to get into the "flow" of the interview** – I personally use this question when I feel distracted going into an interview or I sense that my candidate is not at least 90% in his comfort zone. Non-confrontational opening questions allow both parties to get in sync with one another in preparation for the more complex and

challenging questions (and answers) that will follow.

4. **"Tell me about yourself" gets the candidate talking in a non-structured, open-ended format** – As we've previously discussed, an interview comprised of open-ended questions is the best format for creating a sense of dialogue between the parties. Expert interviewers will begin with this question (or one of its variants) to establish that sense of dialogue. Bear in mind an expert interviewer will also be assessing the candidate's ability to perform in a non-structured setting. Through your answer they will be able to gain a sense of your verbal skills, mental organization, time management and the areas that you feel are important in your background (or why else would you include them in your answer to the initial question?). Your answer to this first question provides an expert interviewer with a significant amount of data that can later be probed for even more data and behaviors. All of this data will then be analyzed to form a judgment about you as a candidate.

For these reasons you can understand how critical your answer to this first question can be. Your answer can form the basis for the first impressions that can last the "lifetime" of the interview. A rambling, unfocused response to this question has facilitated the demise of many an otherwise well-qualified candidate. Because your goal is to help your interviewer close his own mental circle, you will need to give a very powerful "opening statement". If you are successful in doing this, you will find your interviewer going into mental overdrive to convince himself that he made the right decision in the first place when he decided to bring you in for an interview.

Further, if you give a great answer to this first question—including the key elements of your background and achievements—you'll find your interviewer invariably asking his follow-up questions based directly on the data you've just given him in your response. Delivering an answer filled with "good stuff" in an understandable and easy-to-follow manner, allows you even more time to discuss the positive, achievement-oriented aspects of your background as you respond to his follow-up questions based on that "good stuff". As I have observed in many of my training classes, a properly answered first question such as,

"Tell me about yourself" can generate approximately 10 minutes of exchange between the parties. That represents 10 minutes for you to build positive momentum at the start of the interview. As this momentum builds, you'll begin to notice that your interviewer may attempt to "help" you succeed in subtle ways for the balance of the meeting—if for no other reason than to subconsciously congratulate himself on his wisdom in deciding to invite you in for an interview. If you can maintain this positive flow into his second question, you'll find that this positive momentum will begin to assert itself and will become an almost irresistible force in the interview. When "Mighty Mo" reaches this level, then stopping it is analogous to trying to stop an avalanche with a snow shovel. You are now on your way to interview success!

So, with all this in mind, how do we formulate a winning answer to this crucial first question, "Tell me about yourself?"

THE METHODOLOGY

The first thing to bear in mind is that answering this question is NOT your opportunity to "data dump" or otherwise inundate your interviewer with trivia or anecdotes. All human beings have a finite ability to assimilate and process data—varying with the individual. To enable your interviewer to assimilate and process the data you give him (and <u>not</u> rely on his <u>assumptions</u>) your mission is to provide your interviewer with a structured and time-sensitive response. As an aside, by "structured" I don't mean mechanical or staged. I am referring to answering in a logical and cogent manner. Further, your goal is to provide your interviewer with a response that will enable him to ask follow-up questions or probes to "confirm" the positive data you've just given him— helping him to "close the circle".

Here is the methodology I'd like you to follow for this question (and frankly, for most other questions):

1. **Limit your initial response to 3 minutes!**— Time management is essential in answering this question successfully. I have observed candidates create disaster by giving 7-minute soliloquies as "answers" to this question. With a weak interviewer who is unable to stop this type of filibuster, I've seen candidates ramble on for over 10 minutes. In that time, they baffle, befuddle and brutalize their interviewer with a

dump of data no human being can decipher. In that same time period the candidate has most likely missed all of the non-verbal cues being sent by the interviewer indicating that their answer has placed him on overload. I'm guessing that many people can relate easily to this experience having been on the receiving end of this type of data dump at least once. So why is the 3-minute barrier sacrosanct? The answer again lies in the nature of the human condition.

When asked this question, your interviewer, in essence, has given you "permission" to speak. That permission, while freely given, does have its limits—dependent on the personality, objectives and schedule of the interviewer. From your own personal experience, you will most likely agree that it is very difficult to hold another person's attention longer than 3 minutes—unless you "re-engage" your listener; that is, get him personally involved in the conversation. As an example, think about a lecture or training class you've attended—where the instructor was doing all of the talking. Being honest, you will have to admit that your attention span often wandered—in fact, you may have even gotten bored with the speaker and tuned him out at times. Even the most interesting speaker will eventually lose his audience unless he finds a way to engage his audience. As an aside, while teaching my DePaul or Colorado classes, I am very careful to never speak for more than 3-4 minutes continuously. I stop at that point and ask students questions related to what I was saying or ask for comments or reactions. When working with evening graduate students who have already worked a full day, it is very easy to lose them unless you engage them continuously. You need to closely monitor their "body language" for signs of boredom or detachment. Using this same technique is what I'd like you to consider as you answer the questions asked you.

Back to our instant question ("Tell me about yourself"), throughout your answer, closely observe the body language of your interviewer. That body language will usually tell you all you need to know as to whether you're getting through to him or causing him to lapse into a coma. You can bet if they start fidgeting in their chair, lose eye contact with you, pick up an object on their desk and start "playing" with it (e.g. bending a paperclip) or begin attempting to surreptitiously consult their watch or desk clock, you are beginning to lose your audience. When you observe these signals, it is time to re-engage your interviewer by stopping and asking a question such as, "Is this the type of information that you were looking for?" Doing so will get them back into the game.

A final note on the length of the human attention span to remember is the length of television commercials. Have you ever wondered why a television commercial is typically 30-60 seconds in length? Certainly, during the standard 2-3 minute commercial break an advertiser could choose to run longer commercials. Your first answer is most likely, "The reason why they're a minute or less is because of the cost!" While there is no doubt that the cost of commercial airtime is a factor, believe me the big advertisers (P&G, auto companies, telephone companies, etc.) would be willing to pay the additional cost if they were able to support that cost with a corresponding additional benefit (i.e. increased sales). The reality is that these companies have done extensive and sophisticated consumer testing (focus groups, galvanic skin response, video monitoring, etc.) and have concluded that the human attention span is limited to approximately 2 minutes if the message is not directly related to their primary task (such as returning to the latest episode of "Game of Thrones" or "The Walking Dead."). If these companies, with their sophisticated consumer research and state-of-the art production techniques, have concluded that they cannot hold our attention profitably longer than a minute or two, then what should make us think that we are so stimulating that we can hold another human being's attention for longer than 3 minutes without engaging them in a dialogue? Again, this phenomenon is something I'd like you to consider for not only the interviewer's initial question, but for subsequent questions as well. I know you wouldn't be surprised to learn that the most successful salespeople master this technique very early in their careers. In a real sense, isn't that what you are in this instance—a salesperson engaging in perhaps the most important selling situation in your life?

2. Your 3-minute response should be a chronological overview of your background only—with references to your major accomplishments generated from the pre-work you completed in the "Developing an Action-Oriented Resume" section. You'll want to refer back to your "Success Matrix" and review the section "A Company Would Want to Hire Me Because". This is a perfect opportunity to choose those projects or accomplishments that you feel will highlight the skills and attributes you've already identified as your strengths.

Here is an example of what I mean. Let's assume for a moment that you are an Information Systems professional with 18 years of experience in the field. Your answer should sound something like this:

"I have a total of 18 years of IS experience across a variety of platforms and applications." You should work from the past to the present. Bear in mind, if you have 18 years of experience and have worked for 8 companies during that period, it is going to take too long to cover all of

them in your 3-minute response. In this case it is totally permissible to "lump" the first 5-7 years of your experience in a statement such as, *"As you'll note from my resume, I spent the first 6 years of my career working my way through the programming ranks—primarily in financial systems development."* After fast-tracking through your early career, you should now slow down when describing your current role/company and the one immediately preceding it. You can continue with . . . *"Prior my current role at XYZ Company, I spent two years with ABC Corporation as a Project Leader where I was responsible for the design, development and implementation of large-scale systems."* For this role, include the description of only one project and the business benefit from your resume prework. Finally, bring your interviewer to the present with . . . *"After leaving ABC, I joined XYZ, where for the past 4 years I've been a Manager of Information Systems. In this role I've had the opportunity to work on 2 significant projects . . ."* At this point, go back to the information you generated while developing your high-impact resume. Remember the full, 5-point descriptions of each significant project you put together to create your bullet points? Now is the time to insert the 2 most relevant accomplishments or projects into your answer. Remember to use the "transferability of benefit" style—particularly if you're interviewing outside of your industry. Finally, you should include somewhere in your answer a brief reference to your educational background—but **only** if it includes something significant such as a Top 10 B-school MBA, CPA or other certification, or specialized training that directly relates to the job for which you're interviewing. Otherwise, allow your interviewer to get this information from your resume, or ask a specific question as a follow-up. Your 3 minutes is going to go fast. There's no need to take valuable time dwelling on educational trivia—unless again, you have something significant to report (e.g. MBA from Harvard, Wharton, U of C, etc.).

As you have no doubt noticed, answering this question successfully makes the perfect case for having done your homework in advance. If you prepared well in our Pre-Interview Preparation section, then answering questions such as "Tell me about yourself" is a simple function of "plugging in" the work you've already completed.

Be careful not to include more than 4 of your resume "bullets" in this answer or you will overload your interviewer's ability to process the data. This is a perfect case for Nobel Laureate, Dr. Milton Friedman's statement (and the title of his great book) that "small is beautiful".

Remember, your mission is not to "oversell" or to perform a data dump when answering this question. You don't want to be perceived as trying too hard. Instead, give your interviewer a responsive and highly-positive (for you!) answer to his initial question, that will allow him to follow-up with more questions that relate to your strengths.

A great method of concluding your answer to this question is to make a brief reference as to how you "heard" about the opportunity for which you're interviewing. For example, if you were first contacted by a recruiter, you could conclude with, *"And just a week ago I was contacted by the recruiter. He told me about your need for a*

Director. *The way he described both the position and company sounded very interesting! After I did my research, I told him that I was interested and here we are!"* Using this type of ending brings your interviewer (and you) back to the real-time present. This allows the interviewer to move naturally to his follow-up questions pertaining to the information you provided in your "Tell me about yourself" answer, or to move into the usual next area of discussion, "Why would you leave your current position?"

As an aside, please remember to refrain from any "editorial commentary" while answering this initial question. Editorial commentary includes your opinions on co-workers or bosses, company policies or practices with which you disagree, long histories of the companies you've worked for, or company anecdotes or trivia that only a fellow employee would understand and find interesting. Your goal is to stay focused on your work history and key accomplishments in a logical order.

QUESTION #2: WHY WOULD YOU (OR DID YOU) LEAVE YOUR CURRENT POSITION?

Or:

- What caused you to consider looking for another position?
- What do you feel you're not getting from your current role?
- What brings you to our company?
- Etc.

This question represents a veritable minefield that a candidate must pass through unscathed. In my experience, this single question is the reason for more candidate rejection than any other question asked on the interview (excluding the "The Most Dangerous Question" which we'll discuss later!). Many candidates have difficulty in answering this question successfully. The reasons behind this, again, lie in the human condition.

Sad as it might seem, most interviewers are by nature seeking "negative" information—that is, the reasons why they should not hire you vs. the reasons why they should hire you. Most interviewers attempt to protect themselves against the consequences of a "bad hire" by assuring themselves that a candidate does not have any "skeletons in his closet". As a consequence, interviewers will probe this area very carefully indeed; as they don't want to hire someone who is leaving a company for the very same conditions that will be present in the interviewer's own company. Most interviewers will assume that there must be "something wrong" with you or your current employer—or why else would you be sitting in their office talking with them about a new job at a different company? Because of this preconception, it is essential that we carefully consider our answer to this question <u>before</u> the interview. Again, this is where the pre-interview preparation you've completed in Section II pays dividends. You'll be referring back to the output of those exercises to provide you with the basis for successfully answering this question.

Let's discuss the most common "reasons for leaving" that cause candidates difficulty when answering the question, "Why would you leave (did you leave) your position?" You can use the discussion surrounding each to answer similar questions asked you on your interview.

1. **Not able to achieve career goals** (e.g. no growth, not enough $'s, peer promoted over me, company not progressive, don't get along with supervisor, etc.)

   Returning to your pre-work, "Planning for the Long-term", you have already completed an exercise that provides the data for answering this question successfully. In this exercise, you have considered the rationale behind leaving your current company. You will need to synthesize that data to formulate a <u>positive</u> response, indicating what you are not achieving (or able to achieve, even long-term) in your current company that would cause you to investigate new opportunities.

2. **Company downsizing or layoff**

   Many candidates feel that simply indicating that they "were caught" in a restructuring or downsizing is enough of an explanation as to why they have left (or are leaving) a particular company. After all, who today hasn't been impacted by this vampire run amok in corporate America over the past 25 years? However, as straightforward and true as this response might be, don't forget that we're dealing with a normally trusting, but in the role of interviewer, slightly paranoid and suspicious individual. The obvious question your interviewer has, whether spoken or unspoken, is: why were you chosen to be laid off or "restructured"? Why were you seen as "expendable"? Were you considered a weak performer? Did you not get along well with your boss or co-workers? Unless you can provide a rationale for being impacted by the downsizing or restructuring, you allow your interviewer to "assume" an answer—which will usually be negative—concerning you or your capability. We'll return to this everyday occurrence when we discuss "The Most Dangerous Question")

To prevent your interviewer from jumping to the wrong conclusion, you will need to have, at the ready, specific and quantifiable data (numbers, percentages, length of service, etc.) that will provide the rationale behind your departure. For example, a possible response to this question might be, *"Because the Board demanded the company achieve profitability, senior management decided to reduce staff by 30%. However, some departments were hit harder than others. In fact, in my department I was among 10 out of 18 people who left the company. Those that the company kept in my department were either long-service employees or very junior types whose salaries were relatively low compared to mine."*

A good illustration of a downsizing and its impact on employees' jobs was the bankruptcy of United Airlines. Although United's financial difficulties did not hit the media until early in 2002, the fact was that United had been laying-off staff for almost 2 years prior to this. With their bankruptcy filing, United accelerated its layoffs. In this last group of to be laid-off employees, I personally knew many exceptional people. Being laid-off in this circumstance is not a reflection on an individual's ability, value or potential—being "selected" is purely a function of economics. Bear in mind that layoffs such as United's are so well publicized that an in-depth explanation is most likely not needed. However, layoffs taking place at the vast majority of companies are not as well publicized. As such, your "reasons for leaving" must include an explanation similar to that given above in its specificity—so as to head-off erroneous speculation.

3. **Termination due to poor performance, personality conflict or other personal issues**

The vast majority of candidates will have legitimate and easily-explained reasons for leaving their companies. However, there will always be instances where the reason behind an individual's leaving their job was the result of having been fired or terminated for "cause". Even in this event, my counsel when answering this question is to be as truthful as possible. However, it is important to carefully "package" your response. The reason for truthfulness is very simple—most companies today thoroughly reference check candidates prior to hire. In fact, most offer letters will usually have language to the effect that "this offer is contingent upon a successful review of your background"—making the offer able to be "pulled back" at any time if your background check comes back as unfavorable. Even after you've resigned your old position and have already started your new job, the offer can still be withdrawn depending on how unfavorable your background check is. Imagine how embarrassing that would be!

Based on my experience, it is likely that the "real" reason behind your leaving will eventually "come out". If you've already accepted the offer and are found to have been less than forthcoming, again, you will be in the highly compromised position of being perceived as having not been quite truthful or in the worst case—a liar. In either case, you lose! The best avenue to take when there is negative information surrounding your leaving, is to approach the matter objectively; very briefly outlining the circumstances and then moving on. Showing honesty in this area will often cause your interviewer to back down—as most people are reticent about "kicking a man when he's down." At the same time, by your honest and dispassionate explanation, you have placed yourself in a position where you are in control of the data being released, not your previous company who may have an ax to grind. If you just roll the dice and hope that nothing negative comes back in your background review, you are gambling that in the near or moderate-term future the "real" story will not be told—this a very big risk! The downside is that when the story is told, it will be told by others, not you—which is not to your advantage. As already indicated, with the disclosure of the "real" reasons why you left your prior company, you could find your offer being withdrawn prior to your start date. In a worst-case scenario, you could even be fired after starting your new job for falsifying information given on your interview or employment application. Even if neither happens, your credibility with your new boss and your new company will have taken a serious hit if you are not factual with this question on the interview.

Being honest in your answer to this question will also gain you "integrity points" in the mind of your interviewer. There isn't a person alive who hasn't failed at some point in their life. If you demonstrate the ability to discuss a difficult separation openly and objectively, you will grow as a person in the perception of your interviewer.

A question I get asked frequently is how "honest" should a candidate be, regarding the negatives of working for their present/previous company or boss during an interview. In short, emotionally "dumping" or piling on the negativity during your answer is not going to be perceived as a positive quality by your interviewer. No potential employer is going to enjoy the experience of listening to you trash your old company or boss. They may think, ". . . but for the grace of God go I." However, they will understand and accept your explanation if you take a business-like approach. If there is bad news regarding your employer or a present/previous boss, then describe the experience. Keep your description objective and minus personal rancor. Remember the line delivered in the movie, *The Godfather*, when Tessio, one of the Corleone Family's top captains (or *Capo regimes*) is being taken out be to "whacked". Tessio said to Tom Hagen, "Tell Mike it was business, never personal. I always liked him." Use this language as a guide when describing your experiences of working for previous companies or previous bosses—regardless of how onerous the experience was.

QUESTION #3:

WHAT TYPE OF POSITION ARE YOU LOOKING FOR?

Or:

- What brings you to our company?
- Why would you want to work for us?
- What is the most important factor behind your seeking to make a move?
- What are you not getting from your current company/role that you think you can get here?
- What would we have to offer you, both compensation and position, to encourage you to join our company?
- Etc.

Like the preceding question, this seemingly "easy" question has confounded many a candidate. Over the course of my recruiting career I have heard the range of candidates—from entry-level to mature executives—fail miserably on this question. By contrast, I have heard truly outstanding answers from new college graduates with limited or no actual work experience. There are two reasons for earning a failing grade on this question. First, the candidate has not done their homework. Second, the candidate's expectations are not realistic or are not those of a mature adult.

Taking on the first reason, I have found that many candidates seem to feel that the answer to this question is so easy and obvious that they don't need to spend sufficient time preparing to answer it. The obvious ploy is "All I have to do is describe the position I'm interviewing for and I win!" Unfortunately, this is not the winning answer. Certainly, describing what "you're looking for" as being in alignment with the job or environment of the company you're interviewing with can be a positive factor—but, only if that is what you truly feel! Employers tend to become suspicious when you begin telling them what they want to hear. So, even if they buy your answer, at best you're going to be placed in the *average* range of candidates. To be average is not our goal! I want you to be viewed as a "high-impact candidate"—that is, a candidate who is perceived superior to all others. We've already discussed the fact that you're not always going to be the best candidate functionally. So, our goal then, is to make certain you're perceived as the best *qualified* candidate based on your professionalism, preparation and potential. To be seen in that light requires you to do your homework and develop your answer to this question from the analysis you performed during your pre-interview preparation.

Referring back to your Corporate Value Systems Analysis), Pre-Interview Questionnaire and Success Matrix, you will find that you have already generated enough data to be able to answer this question in a high-impact manner. The Success Matrix alone will help you articulate the type of company and culture that will provide you with the highest probability of achieving career success; along with what you've already identified are the new skills and experiences you will need to gain to achieve your long-term career plan.

In sum, synthesize and integrate the analysis you have already done to prepare your answer to this question. Having done so, you can then add the elements of the job for which your interviewing. Use the written Position Description provided by the company or a copy of advertisement or internet posting as your source. Add to that the information that you have gained through your pre-interview investigation of the company to round out your answer. The image you want to project to your interviewer is one of a mature candidate who is well-prepared and able to effectively articulate their goals. This is exactly the quality that employers so *desperately* (yes, I do mean desperately—it's truly hard to find great people) seek in the people they bring into their organizations. In fact, isn't this exactly the type of person that you, personally, would like to hire?

A final word on this question . . .

When I've helped candidates prepare for their interviews, I have had a few individuals who have said, "If I tell them what I really want, and they can't provide it, then I'll be talking myself out of a job. I just don't want to be that honest. I really need this job!" My response has always been that if a candidate truly does need the income the job will provide to live or support their family, then "you do what you gotta do." That's reality. However, barring that situation, I say, "So what!" Wouldn't you rather know right up-front that the company you are interviewing with will not be able to provide you with what is truly important to you? Would you rather spend eight months working at the company only to come to a realization that you could have made during the interview process—namely, that the company/role is unsuitable for you and will never help you achieve your long-term goals? Deny yourself the benefit of this thought process and you'll be out searching all over again in 8-12 months—but at that point you will have wasted valuable "career time". As always, I believe in answering questions honestly, but also with an eye to *realism*. A case in point . . . if you're a 4-year senior accountant who has never managed a department or people and you state during an interview that you want to be considered for a Controller position leading a department of 20+, then it's fair to say your short-term goals are going to perceived as unrealistic and in fact, immature. By the same token, if you have held the position of information systems project manager for 15 years without promotion, stating that you now are seeking a CIO position in a major corporation will also be viewed as an unrealistic goal.

To successfully answer this question, you will have to have done your homework and be realistic and mature as you formulate your answer. Consider the feasibility of attaining the short and long-term goals that you intend to articulate. In a real sense, this question is not only important during employment interviews, but also in your everyday life. If you continually re-evaluate your current position in light of the "type of position you are looking for", then you are well on your way to managing your career in a meaningful direction.

QUESTION #4A:
WHAT ARE YOUR STRONG POINTS?

Or:

- What do you feel you do well?
- How are you different than the rest of your team?
- What have been your greatest contributions or achievements?
- Etc.

If you are properly prepared, this question gives you an opportunity to hit a home run on your interview! The key words in the previous sentence, though, are "properly prepared".

When I've asked this question (or its variants) I invariably get a response such as, "My strong points are that I am results-oriented, have excellent leadership skills and have a strong work ethic." There is no doubt that these are excellent qualities that are highly desired by employers. However, something is missing from this answer that lessens the believability of the statement. What do you think it is?

CLAIM STATEMENTS AND FACT STATEMENTS

What is missing is that this answer is filled with only "claim" statements, not "fact" statements supported by evidence. Unfortunately, as claims, they will be perceived by the interviewer as empty and lacking substance unless specific data or events are provided to support them.

To illustrate this point, let me give you an example of a claim statement. Just suppose we were sitting across from one another and I said to you, "I am the greatest golfer in the world!" Would you believe me? You might look me over, gauge my sincerity and then think, "Well, it's possible, but I really can't believe him because he's not given me a shred of evidence to support his statement. After all, I've never even heard of this guy!" Your reaction would be reasonable under the circumstances because I've only made a "claim" and have not supported it with fact.

Now, suppose I said this instead, "I am the greatest golfer in the world. I can say this because I've won 2 consecutive Grand Slams and have beaten Johnson, Spieth and Thomas and Fowler in every head-to-head match for the past 2 years. And, remember that guy Tiger Woods? He's my caddy!" Assuming these statements to be true, would you be more likely to believe me? Of course! Why? Because, I have supported my "claims" with factual data. Additionally, you would be more likely to retain the *fact* that I am the greatest golfer in the world because the facts would now be coupled with my statement in your thought process.

A high-impact candidate converts their claim statements to fact statements by supporting their claims with objective data. Even if a candidate's "claims" are 100% accurate, they're still going to be perceived as hyperbole by the interviewer unless the candidate converts them to fact statements by offering supporting data.

To achieve this important conversion, I suggest that your response to this question should begin like this:

> "I believe my strong points are that I am results oriented and have excellent leadership skills. For example, when I was working for XYZ Corporation I led the biggest new product launch in our company's history . . ."

From this point, you would proceed to demonstrate your "results orientation" through a brief, but focused description of the new product launch and your efforts that support the description of you as results-oriented. Be specific, and use your action-oriented resume as a reference point. However, be careful not to "oversell" or go overboard with minutia. Selling too hard can be as detrimental to your cause as not selling at all.

To prepare for this question, you'll need to return to your action-oriented resume and consult the "bullet-point" descriptions you prepared describing each of your "deliverables". Another great source of data is your Success Matrix. Consider your answers to the section "A Company Would Want to Hire Me Because". This section represents your "strengths".

I would like you to have 3 "strong points" and their supporting data prepared going into every interview. However, we're only going to use 2 of the strong points. Keep one in ready reserve. By having a reserve strong point, you can avoid the "pregnant pause" that can occur when you've given your answer and then the interviewer just looks at you for a moment and asks, "Any others?" Rather than have to frantically scramble for an additional response, you'll have an already prepared, considered answer ready to go. Once again, you will be presenting yourself as a well-prepared and unflappable candidate! As an aside, for most interviews two "strengths", properly delivered, are sufficient. Automatically, dropping a third strength on your interviewer without being asked, may make you seem braggadocios or worse, as if you're trying too hard.

QUESTION #4B:
WHAT ARE YOUR WEAK POINTS?

Or:

- Where could you improve?
- Are there areas in your background that you'd like to develop?
- What type of training do you feel is necessary for you to achieve your long-term goals?
- Etc.

This is a much-used question that on occasion, has driven me to distraction and sometimes even hilarity. The reason for this is not because I find an individual's honest, self-assessment amusing—because we all have weaknesses! What puts the typical answer to this question in the funny category is *because I so rarely* get an honest, self-assessment! Most candidates attempt to play jiu-jitsu with this question and attempt to disguise a strong point as a weak point. A perfect example of such game-playing is a response such as, *"My weak point is that I'm such a hard worker (or perfectionist, or demanding, or quick study, etc.) that I just don't have enough patience at times with those who don't work as hard (or are as smart, or as perfectionist, or set as high standards, etc.) as me."* Another is, *"My weakness is that I can get bored easily. I need to be in an environment that keeps me busy and challenged."* Let's face it, these are not admissions of "weaknesses" but instead clumsy attempts to dodge the question and substitute strengths in the place of true developmental needs. This type of response sounds superficial and canned. As an aside, four of the books I've read regarding how to answer interview questions suggested the above responses as the best answers to the "weak points' question! However, most interviewers view these types of answers as being non-responsive at best and disingenuous at worst.

My proposal is that you use the candidate's "secret weapon" in answering this question. This weapon will cement your place in the pantheon of high-impact candidates. That secret weapon is . . . honesty! Now before we get started, let me state that "honesty" does not mean beating yourself up or wearing a hair-shirt on the interview. Honesty simply means mature self-assessment.

To begin, you will want to identify two areas in which you feel you could improve. You've already identified these in your Success Matrix in the section, "To Meet My Long-Term Goals I must Gain These Skills/Experiences". This section will give you ample fodder for answering this question. Like the "strong points" question you won't be using both, but instead, you'll be using only 1 developmental need during the interview. Unless of course, you're asked for more, and then you have another ready to go—no fumbling or blurting something out for which you've not has a chance to mentally prepare. **Important note**: Your answer to this question should always take the form of "I'm aware of, and am working on improving." You should never respond by stating, "My weak point is . . .". This only confirms a negative in the mind of your interviewer. Using, "my weak point is" leads your interviewer into assuming that if he hires you, he's stuck with that quality forever! In fact, you should never use the words "weak points" at all. You will want to use the phrase, "an area that I've been *working on* _developing_ is . . .". I'll give you an illustration of how this works by using an example from my own personal experience.

Early in my career I had the decided tendency to over-commit. That is, I would take on more responsibility than I could reasonably be expected to handle or I would commit to an earlier delivery date than was possible. While this characteristic always made my bosses happy at the outset, ultimately that happiness would turn to disappointment when I failed to deliver. This tendency also had the capacity of generating another, equally damning quality—that is, being late. I would be late to meetings, late to work, late coming home for dinner, etc.—all because of my tendency to over-commit. After more than a few disconnects (I was not a particularly quick study in this area), I finally recognized my blind-spot and began working on placing realistic, attainable limits to what I committed. In the midst of this transformation, I can still remember interviewing with PepsiCo and being asked the question, "What are your weak points?" I could have honestly replied, _"My weak point is my tendency to over commit."_ However, I didn't. My response was one I'd like you to consider as you prepare to answer this question on your own interviews. I responded by saying, *"An area that I've been <u>working on developing</u> is my tendency to over commit."* The difference between the two responses may seem subtle on the surface. However, the difference in the type of candidate and person that my interviewer perceived me to be was huge!

By being willing to "give something up", I did the unexpected in the mind of my interviewer. As my interviewer later told me, I gave him real insight into me as a person and established myself as credible—all because I was willing be honest about my developmental needs. However, the key piece of my answer in this interviewer's mind was that I not only recognized that I had a weakness, but that I was already <u>working on improving</u> it.

The advantage to using this language ("an area I'm working on developing") is that you not only gain the integrity "high ground", but you also demonstrate your maturity and desire for self-improvement by committing yourself to improving the developmental need (weak point). This is a much stronger method of answering this question then just saying . . . "My weak point is". Again, while you may get points for honesty (by saying, "My weak point is . . . ", your answer will lead your interviewer to believe that if he hires you, he will be stuck with that weak point forever. Far better to talk about how you have been working to effect self-change and improvement; while at the same time giving your interviewer the hope that what may be a current "developmental need" (that is weakness) may yet develop into a strength.

To summarize—by performing an honest, self-assessment of your capabilities and developmental needs you can craft an answer to this question that will add credibility to everything that you've said before and after your answer. The surprising thing about honesty is that it is always unexpected—and as a result, surprising!

I propose that you adopt this strategy on your own interviews. Again, your goal is not to beat yourself up, but instead to gain the benefits that an honest self-assessment provides. The example I gave was related to one of my own *personal* weaknesses. However, equally acceptable, and probably more advisable, is making reference to *professional* or *skill-based* areas needing development. Examples are:

- More experience leading people
- Greater knowledge of a particular functional area (e.g. cost accounting)
- Need for additional education (MBA, MS, PhD, etc.) or certification (e.g. CPA, SPHR)
- More experience in international business
- Etc.

Any of these developmental areas, or their like, could appear on your Success Matrix in the Developmental Section and are suitable for use when answering the "weak points" question.

QUESTION #5:
WHERE DO YOU SEE YOURSELF IN 5 YEARS?

Or:

- What are your long-term goals?
- Where do you see your career taking you?
- What jobs or roles do you aspire to?
- Do you see yourself as a "generalist" or a "specialist" long-term?
- Etc.

This, the last of "The 5 Questions", is more often than not, your last opportunity to create a high-impact perception in the mind of the interviewer. Interestingly enough, while virtually every interview will include this question, only a very small handful of interviewers will ask this question for the right reasons <u>and</u> be able to render accurate judgments on you as a candidate based on your response.

Your response to this question will give an expert interviewer insight not only into your career plan and "drive" (the standard reason for asking the question), but also your maturity, judgment, planning ability and level of self-awareness. Expert interviewers will consider your answer in the context of whether your goals are reasonable given the abilities you've shown to date. They will consider the environment and culture of their firm/client and overlay those onto your response in an attempt to gauge the likelihood of your achieving your long-term plan. In the hands of an expert interviewer, you give up a significant amount of information about yourself when you answer this question. However, if you are well prepared for this question you get a chance to really hit a rocket out of the park!

However, even with interviewers of lesser ability we need to be able to answer this question well. Unfortunately, a non-expert interviewer's inability to fully understand and place your response in the proper context can cause him to jump to erroneous conclusions—seriously damaging your chances of receiving an offer. More on this topic as you read on.

For both types of interviewers, we need to return to our homework to develop a high-impact response to this question. The "Pre-Interview Questionnaire" and "Planning for the Long Term" can supply the basis for your answer. Carefully study your answers to the questions in both exercises before you prepare your response. Consider the *level* (vs. the Job Title) of the job to which you aspire. Better to say that your goal is to lead the HR function than to say that you want to be VP HR. The title "VP" may not be the most senior role or perhaps the interviewer aspires to that same title himself. Also, is your goal to become the top functional expert in a chosen specialty (e.g. Director of Compensation) or to become the top generalist in your function (e.g. VP Human Resources)? Or, do you aspire to general management (e.g. CEO)? Consider also, whether you might opt for a "career shift" at some point in your life, or a change in your field of endeavor (e.g. from manufacturing to marketing or sales). As a mental challenge, I always encourage my candidates to consider the last job they would like to hold just prior to retirement from the corporate workforce. With that understanding you could use your corporate career to better prepare you for what you really want to do after retirement (we'll talk about Lou Brock in just a second). Or, you could use your corporate experience to launch an entrepreneurial career. Why not do your learning on someone else's nickel?

With regard to career shifting, my favorite example is Hall of Fame Left Fielder, Lou Brock of the St. Louis Cardinals. In 1964, in one of baseball's all-time bonehead moves, my semi-beloved Cubs traded Lou Brock to St. Louis for a sore-armed pitcher, Ernie Broglio. Lou went on to become one the greatest left-fielders ever and earned a pedestal in Cooperstown. When he left baseball, he made a significant career shift—he became a florist! Without a doubt these were two very different career paths—each drawing on different skills. The game of baseball requires competitiveness, aggression and physical skills. The role of a florist requires creativity, patience and vision, plus solid business skills. You may decide to follow a path similar to Lou Brock's and make a significant career shift at some point. Why not consider what "this" might be when you're preparing to answer this question. What you uncover might put you on the path to achieving that goal. However, this type of insight regarding "far in the future" career shifts, is for your edification only. You need to be pragmatic in developing your answer to this question for a job interview. Telling a hard-core, VP Finance that your long-term goal is to become a "Florist" might cause him to view you as a resident of the planet, Mongo! As always, your response to this question should be honest, but also be in alignment with the venue you are in—namely, an employment interview!

Finally, because we're in this for the long-term, I'd like you to consider your present career direction and options. Evaluate the position that you currently hold, and the position you're likely to move into next. Are they supporting and facilitating your movement in the career direction you've chosen? I fully appreciate that your goals and "end game" may change over time based on your personal and professional experiences. It is for this reason that it is important to monitor your progress towards your long-term goals regularly to make certain that you are staying "on track" and not burning valuable career time on "dead ends".

As in the first question, when developing your response to this question, remember our 3-minute target. By this point in your interview, you'll have established a dialogue and built rapport with your interviewer. You would not want to damage or erode that rapport at the end of the interview by delivering an unfocused, incoherent or unrealistic soliloquy about your plans for the future. Most interviewers—despite the fact that this question clearly relates to the future—are only concerned about the here and now; that is, how you can help them in the short-term. Belaboring the future is not going to impress your interviewer. The key element is to demonstrate that you have actually thought through your future career path and that you do indeed have a plan. That plan, while critically important to you, will never reach the same level of importance in the mind of your interviewer.

FINAL THOUGHTS ON "THE FIVE QUESTIONS"

As you have no doubt concluded, one of the recurring themes in our discussion of *"The Five Questions"* has been honest self-assessment. I know there are people who will disagree with me and state that it is to a candidate's advantage to stay with "safe", non-confrontational answers; that is, answers that tell the interviewer exactly what they want and need to hear. However, as you consider the degree to which you want to apply that honest self-assessment in your responses, I ask you to ponder the words of the very funny Groucho Marx. When asked why he wasn't interested in joining a particular country club, Groucho replied, "I wouldn't join any club that would have me as a member!" Paraphrasing Groucho, I say, "Any company that would not hire me because of what or who I am, I wouldn't want to work for anyway!"

Before you reject that statement, consider how much time is spent either at, or related to, your job. In addition to the actual time spent at work, there is the time spent thinking about work from the moment you wake, showering, commuting to/from work, the time spent working at home in the evenings, etc. Even our weekends are not free of our jobs and companies as very often those we socialize with are co-workers. In short, the majority of our waking hours are spent thinking about our jobs. Who knows, maybe even our dreams, too! If a job is not working well for you, it can seriously blacken every other aspect in your life. If "talking" yourself into a job and company that is not right for you creates unhappiness in your work life, then it is likely that the other parts of your life will suffer as well. I know this sounds trite, but I always encourage my candidates to consider the words of Polonius in Shakespeare's, *Hamlet* . . .

"To thine own self be true and it must follow as night does the day thou can'st not be false to any man."

So, now that you have a template for your interview, let me emphasize again, the importance of practice and rehearsal before the interview. With practice your interview performance will be perceived as natural and open. Without practice and under the pressure of the interview, you may come across as stiff and canned; or, even worse, make serious verbal blunders that torpedo your chances of receiving an offer. Remember our discussion on winning NFL coaches. They never send their teams onto the field on Sunday without having practiced the week before. In those practice sessions, the coach will run the same play over and over again until he feels that every player totally understands their responsibilities and how they should react. In that manner, in the heat of battle, when there are the pressures of 60,000 screaming fans and a game on the line, his team can execute the play without error. It is this preparation and practice that makes for both winning football teams and high-impact candidates!

THE MOST DANGEROUS QUESTION:

Now that we've discussed The Five Questions you probably feel that you are ready for anything; and, at this point there is absolutely no question that could cause you difficulty. Sorry to say, but there is one more question that we haven't discussed—and in fact, it is the most dangerous question of all. Every candidate must be aware of its presence and be ready to respond to it; or, risk the high probability of being rejected as a candidate. In fact, this single question has been responsible for more candidate rejection than any other question in my recruiting career. What is this dreaded question you ask?

The most dangerous question involved in any employment interview is:

THE QUESTION NOT ASKED!

What makes this "question" so dangerous is that the candidate never gets a chance to respond to the interviewer's unspoken concern. Specifically, the interviewer is either consciously or subconsciously bothered by something a candidate said (or didn't say), but he never asks a question to clarify or answer his concern—he simply *assumes* an answer for the candidate. Making assumptions without facts can be very dangerous to us as candidates. Have you ever been given the reason being for rejected for a position because you: ". . . wouldn't have been interested in the role long-term"; or, because you ". . . would be too senior for the role"; or, ". . . you are probably seeking more money than we can pay"; etc.? If so, then you have experienced, first-hand, the negative impact of this very dangerous (non) question. In each instance, the company's interviewer/s simply assumed an answer based on their own value system—not the candidate's. Again, to compound matters, they most likely never asked the candidate follow-up or clarifying questions that might have led to a different understanding and ultimately a different outcome!

Over the course of my recruiting experience, I have observed hundreds of hiring managers and HR professionals commit this most unforgivable offense in a hiring situation; that is, making a decision based on presumption rather than fact.

Lest you get too confident about your own background (as in: "My background is totally clean! No one could jump to a false conclusion about me!"), bear in mind that everyone has *something* in their past, profile or skill set that could cause an interviewer to mistakenly send them down the candidate's black hole. As a consequence, everyone must be prepared for this eventuality. To underscore this point, I'd like to share an event that took place a few years ago. It takes a bit of space to tell, but you'll find it worth reading.

I was conducting a VP of Credit and Collections search for a large technology firm. This was a search for a $200K+ individual. I only mention the salary level to point out that the level of a search does not immunize it from errors caused by making assumptions. Even at the most senior levels the errors caused by making assumptions (vs. verifying facts) can be significant.

Our final candidate was truly outstanding. She had over 20 years of direct experience, had been a key executive and mover in a firm that had grown from $400mm to $10B over a nine-year period, and had references that were among the best I've ever taken. In short, she was uniquely positioned to make a major contribution to my client. She did not receive an offer. She was rejected for reasons that left me not at all speechless.

The reason for her rejection was that she "failed" the routine credit and background investigation. This client utilized an outside, 3rd party firm to verify educational credentials, credit and criminal history.

In the course of their investigation the background checking firm uncovered the "fact" that my candidate's social security number was also being used by another person (in fact, a former co-worker) on a real-estate transaction—implying some sort of real-estate fraud. Also, the background checking firm had been "unable" to verify her degree status. These two issues were seen as "misrepresentations" of data she had provided on her employment application. Based on this, my client opted to reject her at the 11th hour—despite having told the candidate the prior day that she would be receiving an offer.

I was, to say the least, quite upset for three reasons. First, I suspected that somehow mistakes had been made on the background check and no attempt had been made to verify the information. Second, because the company's recruiter (who seemed to have his own agenda) was not willing to consider the real, factual evidence the candidate was able to produce—specifically, a photocopy of her diploma. Third, because the candidate and I were totally "blindsided"—we had no inkling that a problem in her background check existed until we were told she was being rejected for a role that just 24 hours earlier she had been assured by the company would be hers.

Here's the reality of the two "misrepresentations":

I personally called the Regional U.S. Social Security Administration (SSA) office and found that there was no possible way that the background checking firm could have gotten information about a "shared" Social Security number. The simple fact is that the SSA will only *verify* a very limited amount of information about the cardholder. They will not discuss or volunteer any information regarding a cardholder. They will verify only, full name, date of birth and Social Security number. And significantly, you must provide the information in these three areas and they will only tell you if it is correct or incorrect—that's it! This strict policy is in place to protect the privacy of the individual and to prevent identity theft. In short, it was impossible for the background checking service to have gotten information regarding a "shared" social security number from the SSA. So how did they uncover this damaging "revelation"?

The answer is ineptitude and carelessness. About 4 years earlier my candidate had made a real estate investment with a former co-worker. Both of their names and Social Security numbers were listed on the title of a particular house as is necessary with dual-owner investment properties. In this case, the background checking firm didn't go far enough in their investigation. The background checking firm presumed they had uncovered a "shared" Social Security number when they performed a *Property Search* on the internet—unfortunately, they didn't scroll far enough into the document to display her co-worker's Social Security number. And, very troubling, they did <u>NOT</u> check with the SSA (as they had indicated they had to my client) to verify the authenticity of my candidate's social security number.

Regarding their inability to verify her degree, the reason was also easily uncovered by my conducting a very simple piece of detective work. I asked my candidate the question! As it turned out, my candidate had attended a small, private college in the U.K., graduating in 1980. In 1988, that college was acquired by and absorbed into a large, London-based university—hence, the name of the private college was no longer used. When I questioned my candidate, she informed me of her school's name change as a result of the acquisition. A quick call by me to the registrar of the acquiring University completely verified the candidate's degree status. As mentioned earlier, she also had a copy of her diploma which we had faxed to my client—but to no avail.

In both of these areas of "factual misrepresentation", shoddy work by an outside background checking service and the unwillingness of my client to ask follow-up questions resulted in a truly outstanding candidate not getting an offer. As an aside, upon this candidate's rejection, the role was then offered to the #2 candidate, a former colleague of the CEO. Simply challenging these erroneous assumptions by asking questions would have revealed the inaccuracies that ultimately caused my candidate to be rejected.

Was there an unhappy ending to this story? Yes! However, it is the moral to this story that should concern us. The moral to this story is that we must be prepared to respond to, and answer the "most dangerous question". We can't ignore it or pretend it doesn't exist. To do either is to invite disaster! So how do we prepare to answer this most dangerous question—the question not asked? To prepare, you will have work to do before, during and after the interview.

The first step is to objectively, not defensively, review your resume before your interview. Consider your job changes and the reasons behind them. Assess the length of service at each company—if there were "short stops" (less than 1 year), then be prepared to explain why. Don't assume that your interviewer knows that you left a company because of a well-publicized downsizing—because he may just assume you were fired for incompetence. If you have made several lateral or even "backwards" moves title-wise, be prepared to explain that, too. Make certain that your interviewer completely understands the rationale behind a title change that might appear as a lateral or even backwards move if the titles are a function of company size. For example, being a "Manager" at a $5B company is most likely a bigger role than being a "Director" at a $5mm firm. However, you'll need to be ready with an explanation so as to prevent someone from assuming that you are "not promotable" because of the lateral or backwards progression shown on your resume. Be certain that every bit of information on your resume (and as important, the employment application) can be verified easily. Check with your references to make certain they are aware that someone may be contacting them and that they've agreed to provide information regarding you.

Remember, the vast majority of interviewers you encounter are not going to be pros and like any other human being can be prone to interviewer bias and mistaken assumptions—if we let them.

I recommend that you ask a trusted colleague (*not* a spouse, etc.) to objectively review your resume and then offer their comments and perceptions. You'll need to defer any defensiveness that you might feel from their critique. In effect, they'll just be voicing the same concerns that a hiring manager/recruiter might have about your background, but *won't* tell you!

The second step in preventing the most dangerous question from sinking you takes place during the interview itself. Watch your interviewer carefully for their reactions to your responses. If you sense that they are less than satisfied with, or have formed a negative opinion from your response, or if you feel you didn't provide a key element of data in your answer, RESIST at all costs the natural tendency to play dodge ball with their unspoken question—or pretend that it doesn't exist. It does exist and could possibly come back to haunt you unless you address it head on. This often happens with "sensitive" questions, such as why a candidate left a company after a short period of time. In some cases, there are negative reasons as to why a candidate left. However, in that scenario, wouldn't you rather be in the position to engage the issue and have control over the "spin" placed on the event—rather than having your interviewer make their own assumptions and placing their own spin on the event—potentially ending your candidacy?

The third and final means of guarding against the "most dangerous question" takes place after the interview. Critique your own performance (we'll discuss this in detail in the next section "Decision Time"). If you feel there were areas where incorrect assumptions could have been made, respond to them directly when you write your follow-up "thanks for the interview" email; or communicate these concern to your recruiter (if you are working with one) so that he can use your input to overcome potentially damaging objections before they have a chance to pick up too much momentum and become unstoppable.

To re-emphasize—of the many questions asked during the course of an interview, there is no more dangerous question than the question not asked!

SECTION V – DECISION TIME

With the toughest phases of your candidacy now complete, you are ready to move into the third and final phase of the recruiting process—decision time. Note that I did not use the term "offer time". The reason is that an offer is only the output of decisions made—both by you and the company. You play a vital role in this phase of the process given that you must decide to accept or reject any offer made. And, if an offer is not made, you must still decide how to move forward with your job search. Specifically, what lessons have you learned from your interview that can improve your next performance? What changes could you make in your preparation or presentation so as to better generate a job offer from the next company with whom you meet?

POST-INTERVIEW SELF-DEBRIEF:

After you've concluded the interview, take the time necessary to review and critique your performance. Consult the notes you have taken. Consider your interviewer's reactions to you as a candidate. Consider your own reactions to what you heard, saw and felt. Don't wait too long after your meeting to conduct this self-debrief, because given the human condition, your memory will lapse or you may begin to "gloss over" seemingly insignificant comments made by the interviewer that may be very important indications of how they are feeling about you as a candidate or what it would be like to work for the company. The key questions you must be able to answer at this point are:

1. Did I feel comfortable with the people that I met? Could I work with or for them?
2. Do I have enough information about this opportunity to make an informed decision?
3. Does this role meet the requirements I pre-defined in my Success Matrix?

And most important . . .

4. Am I interested enough in the opportunity to move to the next step in the process—either additional interviews or an offer?

Being able to answer these questions at every step of the process is essential to good decision-making—that is, a decision you can commit to and having made, live happily with. All too often, candidates give these important questions no serious consideration until they receive an offer—then they want a week or longer to begin the thought process of making up their mind. I believe this is the wrong approach. If you are invited back for a second interview, you can be sure that the company's interest in you is more than casual. That's the point at which to start seriously considering the opportunity. If you decide that the role is not for you or that whatever the company might offer would not be sufficient, then stop the process! Don't continue to burn interview time on a role that you know after the first meeting is not right for you. Conversely, if you are interested in the role after the first interview, then this self-assessment will help you to prepare relevant questions and areas to be explored during the next meeting. Knowing what your issues are, you'll be able to meet them head-on during the next interview vs. waiting until after an offer is made and then attempting to confront an unresolved issue—or worse, being forced to make a decision with incomplete data.

SENDING "THANK YOU" LETTERS

As a matter of common courtesy, a "Thank You" letter should be sent to every member of the interview team. Normally, this is going to involve making certain that you've obtained an email address or business card from those on the team. However, as a high-impact candidate, your Thank You letter is going to be a bit different than the usual, "Thank you for the time spent interviewing me, I'm interested in the job." letter that interviewers receive as a matter of course. While we do want to recognize the efforts and time spent by our interviewers, we also want to use the Thank You letter as one more opportunity to demonstrate our qualifications for the job. So, how do we do this?

Remember, that we've already discussed the necessity of taking notes during your interviews—those notes will generate the core of your letter. For example, let's suppose that your interviewer was the Controller, we'll call her Mary. During that conversation, Mary mentioned the high growth of the company and how in the midst of that growth, her department was charged with the implementation of the SAP financial module. Further, she indicated that one of the reasons why she was interested in meeting with you is because of your experience with SAP. With this scenario in mind, here's what a Thank You letter to Mary should look like:

Dear Mary,

Thanks for the time spent meeting with me, Tuesday. I really enjoyed our conversation and your description of the growth taking place at XYZ

Corporation. Having now had a day to consider our conversation, I find myself very interested in the role.

During our meeting you mentioned the SAP Financials implementation that is currently underway in the midst of significant growth. Having had a similar experience as the SAP Implementation Project Manager with my current firm, ABC Company, I am well aware of the challenges ahead for you and your team. In fact, the opportunity to make an immediate contribution to your SAP implementation is one of the many things that has really sparked my interest in this role.

Again, thank you for meeting with me. I look forward to the opportunity to talk with you again.

   Sincerely,

As you'll note, the first and last paragraph are plain vanilla. They appear in virtually all Thank You's. However, it's the middle paragraph that will cause Mary to think back to her interview with you and remember your SAP experience positively.

The key to a high-impact Thank You letter is personalization, brevity and timing.

First, to be personalized, you'll need to have taken notes while meeting with every member of the interview team and recorded what their "hot buttons" seemed to be during their meeting with you. Based on those notes, you'll be able to insert a personalized "middle paragraph" into your Thank You letter. This is very important, as again, we're using the Thank You letter not only to be polite, but also to sell our backgrounds. Each Thank You sent should include a personalized middle paragraph and how you are uniquely qualified to address the need identified by your interviewer in it.

Second, brevity is important. I've seen candidates send Thank You that were 2 pages long. Let's be honest, that's selling a bit too hard, don't you think. Not only that, but doing so is completely unnecessary. You get infinitely more impact from a 3 paragraph, *Readers Digest* version Thank You, such as illustrated above, than you do with the *War and Peace* version that many candidates feel is necessary. Don't forget, the reader has to actually read the letter, and the longer it is, the more time it takes to read. Also, too much information puts your reader in "information overload" mode and being there is not where we want our reader to be. Net: Your email should be short, and not exceed 3 brief paragraphs (approximately 100 words).

Finally, the timing of when the interviewer receives the email is important. There are some candidates who go home or back to their office and immediately fire off an email to their interviewer. Others will wait 4-5 days and then send their letter. In my opinion, the first example is too soon, and the other too late.

I recommend that you send your Thank You email, either late in the evening the day of the interview, or the very first thing the day after. This will cause your email to be waiting for your interviewer when they log onto their computer the next morning. Because it will be in the "morning load", there's a better chance that they'll read it immediately, vs. the email that arrives at 2:00 pm during the heat of the afternoon crunch. Remember, we're trying to create perceptions at every step of the process. By waiting that extra time, you are sending a very subtle signal that: A) You are a thoughtful individual—you don't act impulsively, you like to consider issues. B) You have been thinking about the job for at least 12 hours and still have an interest in the position. An additional benefit of waiting that extra time, is that you don't let you interviewer forget about you. The candidate who sends his Thank You letters immediately after the interview, fires off all of his guns at one time—and allows the interviewer's memory of him to fade after 24 hours. By holding just that extra day, you get a chance to put your name right back into the consciousness of your interviewer—in a very positive way. By contrast, those candidates who wait 4-5 days to send their Thank You's are now attempting to connect with someone whose detailed memory of the interview has probably faded—as almost a week has passed. During that week, they've potentially interviewed other candidates and most certainly have had a full plate of "work thoughts" to further dim their memories of the interview.

So, make certain to send a Thank You to your interviewers; but, also remember the importance of personalization, brevity and timing.

USING YOUR RECRUITER EFFECTIVELY

If you have worked with an executive recruiter to obtain the interview, then call him and give your open and honest feedback. Remember, the recruiter's goal is to place you. They *want* to place you! Providing your recruiter with detailed feedback is a vital step in assuring they have the necessary data to overcome potential or real objections by the client. A good recruiter is experienced in overcoming client objections, but only if they have sufficient data from you to do so.

Often candidates are reluctant to share information with recruiters because they feel they have to "play their cards close to the vest." This approach could prove to be costly should your recruiter be "blindsided' by a client objection based on something that was discussed with you, or worse, a client's assumption (i.e. a question not asked), and be unable to deliver a counter-argument because they lack information. It is too late to give your recruiter this insight after the client has rejected you as a candidate. At that point the client's perceptions are no longer perceptions in their mind. They have hardened and become facts. Just remember, with regard to your recruiter . . . you're both on the same team.

At the same time, you should expect feedback from the company via your recruiter. Don't be shy about asking for feedback from your recruiter. You'll need this information to help you decide about next steps.

YOU'VE RECEIVED AN OFFER!

Congratulations!

There is no doubt that one of life's greatest feelings is receiving a job offer—particularly when that offer is for a job that you really want! In a business sense, a job offer is a candidate's ultimate self-validation in terms of their ability, potential and personality. You'll notice I used the word "candidate" vs. "employee". An employee's greatest validation is getting promoted! It is now time for celebrating and receiving the heartfelt congratulations of your family and the best wishes of your peers . . . right? Uh . . . not!

While I always congratulate my candidates upon receiving an offer (as it represents a victory over the process) I also caution them that there is still real work to be done. Specifically, there is a need to answer many questions. Does the offer make sense? Does the company match up against the culture and environment best suited for you to achieve success? Will your new boss have a sincere interest in advancing your career? Will there be a proper balance between your ability to learn new skills and contribute to the company? Is the compensation (including the benefit program) sufficient to financially support a decision to accept the offer? All of these questions, and more, must be answered before a candidate is capable of intelligently accepting or rejecting a job offer. When you receive an offer, the decision that you make is going to have potentially far-reaching consequences for you—both professionally and personally. Why not take sufficient time to again, do your homework before you take the test? The good news, though, is that if you have been following the program, you have already done most of that homework.

Beyond the on-going "checks" that you have been performing as you have gone through the process (as discussed in "Post-Interview Debrief") I suggest you return to your Success Matrix. Begin to "plug in" the data you have gained from your interview/s against each of the boxes containing your pre-defined criteria. Does this new company meet the standard you've set for "Culture/Environment? You have already identified your areas of strength in your Success Matrix ("A Company Would Want to Hire Me Because"). Will this new role play to your strengths? If so—how? And if not—is there the potential that future jobs in the company will allow you to leverage those strengths? Regarding your identified long-term goals, will the new company offer you a platform that will allow you to achieve them or, at a minimum, can the company provide you with new skills and experiences that will help you attain your career goals with a different company?

Receiving an offer is the payoff for all the hard work you've already invested. That hard work now gives you the ability to make an informed, logical decision. As an aside, being logical does <u>not</u> mean that you ignore your emotions totally. Receiving a job offer is a business proposition to be sure—however, it should also create an emotional high. You're supposed to be excited and happy! This emotional element is a good thing, too! Without the emotional kick an offer generates, the job search process with all its attendant hard work would not be fun! Receiving an offer is tantamount to your new boss saying, "I want you! We can't run this business without you! You're needed here!" These are pretty heady feelings, indeed!

Therefore, I don't want you to totally ignore the emotional element, but only to manage it well. Place your focus on thoroughly analyzing the opportunity using the criteria for success you've established before the process began—when you were objective, rational and unengaged from the tumult of receiving a job offer.

This tumult exists with every offer and for every person regardless of level. Whether you've received an offer for CEO or an entry-level job in production, you're going to feel your emotions. Even big-time CEO's get excited when they receive offers! I'll bet that even Steve Jobs was excited when he was offered the opportunity to return to Apple in 1996 as CEO, after having been fired from the job 10 years earlier. Don't think that you are totally immune from your emotions, either.

My goal for you is that whichever decision you make (accept or reject) should be one that you can live with happily over time. The odds of achieving this goal tilt heavily in your favor when you utilize an objective, rational approach to your decision-making process.

At this point, we need to return to one of our earlier discussions. What if this job, company and offer are not perfect? What if this role does not meet all of the criteria you've set? My counsel is that now is the time to objectively assign priorities to the various elements of the offer, job and company. As we have discussed, it is not likely that every objective you've set will be met. We rarely get everything we want. Only you can decide which elements of the offer are "deal breakers" and which are those that can be compromised. Consider these carefully.

If this opportunity does present hurdles, or obstacles, then your responsibility—as a candidate and adult—is to attempt to remove them. This means you cannot wait for the company to play mind reader—you must be prepared to identify and elevate your concerns to the company. Your task is to develop a list of your concerns and corresponding proposals to remedy those concerns and then present this list to the company. If this is an offer that you'd like to accept, but for an issue or two, then you must take these issues back to the company—either directly or through your recruiter (if you're using one). This is not the time to keep them hidden. I have known candidates who did not articulate their concerns before accepting an offer and just hoped for the best—and lived to regret not having done so. Conversely, I have had candidates reject offers without presenting their rationale to the company only to find out, after the fact, that their concerns could have been resolved to their satisfaction had they just communicated their issues. The bottom line is that to make a good decision (either accepting or rejecting) you must eliminate as much of the unknown as possible. Only by raising the issues and getting answers can you do so.

HOW MUCH TIME SHOULD I TAKE TO MAKE MY DECISION?

I am asked this question frequently by my candidates. While I am never in favor of making instant decisions about important matters, I also feel that an accept/reject decision is like fruit—it only stays ripe for a while and then goes bad! An employment decision that takes too long to make, goes rotten—and can leave a foul taste in the mouths of all parties concerned. The appropriate amount of time to wait is as long as it takes you to complete your analysis, plus one night. I support "sleeping" on your decision. After you've made your decision, go to bed that evening. If you still feel the same when you wake the next morning, then call the company immediately and announce your decision. Call your recruiter, too—keep him in the loop. And . . . for your own mental health, once you've made a decision, stick with it! As previously discussed, this type of decision can cause your emotions to roil—particularly if there is a geographic relocation involved or it causes some other significant change in your life. If you've decided to reject the offer, then be prepared to deal with the "what if's" you may feel 6 months later. Like any human being, you may find yourself playing "what if" mind games in the future such as, "What if I'd joined Framistat Corporation, I wouldn't be working for this jerk right now . . ." and so on. Again, my counsel is to make your call, learn from the experience and then leave the soul searching in the past.

If you've decided to accept your offer, you will now have to face the prospect of announcing your resignation to your current boss and co-workers— which can be, short-term, an unsettling experience! I use the word unsettling because it will be after your announcement that your company may decide to pull out the heavy artillery—a counter-offer and its consort, the guilt-trip! And, believe me, companies will play the "guilt-trip" card to the max to encourage you to stick around.

SHOULD YOU ACCEPT A COUNTER-OFFER?

While I was a corporate HR executive I was (all modesty aside) very good at encouraging potentially resigning employees to accept our counter-offers and remain with the company. It used to give me a great sense of satisfaction to enter the game in the bottom of the 9th inning and earn a "save". I had this sense of satisfaction until I saw the futility of extending counter-offers. With very few exceptions accepting a counter-offer is *always* in the best interest of the company—and usually not in the employee's long-term best interests. After all, it is going to be time-consuming, expensive and a downright hassle to replace you—not to mention, it's a bit embarrassing to your boss to lose such a terrific performer such as you. Is it any wonder, then, that companies find it cheaper and more expedient to attempt to keep the current employee rather than attempt to find a replacement?

But, here is a very simple, but critical, fact to consider:

ACCEPTING A COUNTER-OFFER IS ULTIMATELY FUTILE

I used to keep statistics of my track record in successfully countering offers. Between the years 1975 and 1985 I *successfully* prevented 28 employees from leaving the companies for which I was working. However, here's the rub—only <u>one</u> of those employees remained with my companies longer than one year after accepting our counter-offer! The remaining 27 ultimately accepted other offers from different companies and left the organization. A few even accepted offers from the company that had initially extended the offer we had "successfully" countered! As a side note, my sole, long-term "success" was a person who was forced to remain with our company due to unique personal circumstances that developed that prevented him from considering offers outside of our headquarters city. And, because we were the only game in town to do what he wanted to do, we were, in the end, his only option.

My message is that once you have prepared a resume, competed in the interview process and received an offer, you are already very far downfield mentally in your decision to leave your current company. In truth, I could give you eight excellent reasons not to accept a counter-offer, but one will suffice. They just don't stick! The circumstances and issues within a company that encouraged you to seek new opportunities initially will always be present in your company. Counter-offers, at best, provide a short-term fix, a band-aid if you will, to the systemic issues that created your initial mindset for looking outside the company. My counsel is to listen and consider every counter-offer. However, unless that counter-offer represents a fundamental, paradigmatic change in the operation or culture of the company or represents a long-lasting redress of your key issues, <u>reject it and move on</u>!

A BIRD IN THE HAND—YOU'VE RECEIVED AN OFFER, BUT YOU HAVE ANOTHER PENDING . . . WHAT DO YOU DO NOW?

A truly exceptional circumstance occurs in the recruiting process when you receive an offer from Company "A" and have another offer in the works from Company "B". I personally love these scenarios because I have always felt that the best decisions are made by candidates with options or alternatives. However, this scenario can present a candidate with a dilemma—namely, how do I keep Company "A" at bay while I wait for an offer from Company "B"?

In my experience, I've had candidates who have played out this game in every conceivable fashion. Based on this experience, I can offer an example of one formula for disaster and one proven formula for success.

First, the formula for disaster is created when a candidate keeps the competing opportunity ("B") a "secret" from Company "A" and their recruiter (if applicable). They receive an offer from "A" and then proceed to delay and delay. They are non-responsive and then, when they receive "B's" offer and decide to accept it, they call Company "A" and announce their rejection.

Needless to say, everyone involved in the process at Company "A" feels quite put upon. The primary reason for this feeling is that the candidate simply did not demonstrate the element of trust in his relationship with Company "A". Trust is a very strong element in any relationship—personal or professional. While the candidate was interviewing with Company "A", this trust relationship grew as the interview process progressed. When "A" extended an offer to our candidate, it was, in a sense, the fulfillment of a trust relationship between the parties. When an offer is extended, the hiring manager particularly, is demonstrating his trust in the candidate's ability to perform successfully as a member of his team.

As we discussed in an earlier section, the hiring manager has a big piece of his own career tied up in the success of the people he hires. Is it any wonder then, that trust is a factor in the offer process? When our candidate, unilaterally opts to reject "A's" offer, and "blindsides" the company with that rejection, he destroys that trust relationship. The hiring team of the Company A is not only disappointed in the candidate's rejection, they're most likely upset as well, because the candidate never gave them an opportunity to respond to the second offer. This is the inverse to *The Most Dangerous Question* discussed earlier. In a sense, "A" can't help but feel "used" because the candidate treated them (in "A's" opinion) in a cavalier manner. In "A's" mindset, the candidate broke the trust that they felt had been established.

Be assured that the candidate who adopts this strategy will have "burnt the bridge" with Company "A". More important, he has potentially damaged his future relationship with those involved with the offer. To the extent that these individuals will most likely join other companies in the future, this could be problematic for the candidate longer-term. Every company—just as every candidate—has known rejection. They can handle it! However, the candidate who delivers a blindside rejection to a firm breaks the trust element with the hiring manager and the hiring team. He may even place the hiring manager in the embarrassing position of not only losing "his candidate", but also being caught unawares and having to explain both to his boss.

If you find yourself in the lucky position of having an offer in hand and waiting for a second (or third!), my suggestion is to fully communicate your options with the company extending the first offer (again, Company "A"). Who knows, by doing so you may even cause Company "A" to sweeten their offer as a preemptive strike. At a minimum you have treated the company and its hiring team with respect. My counsel, however, is that while you can tell Company "A" during the interview process that you have other possibilities (only if in fact you do), do not get definitive until you have received their offer in writing. Without that written confirmation, Company "A" might just decide that it is not worth the chase or wait, and go to their second choice. Get the offer in writing first, then, communicate fully.

Be advised that when you communicate your other options to Company "A", they may begin to apply pressure on you to decide quickly—so as to obviate the possibility of Company "B's" offer even being extended.

This is done by "time bounding" the offer; that is, indicating that the offer is only "good" for a limited time (usually 5 business days). In such a case, here is a proven formula for buying yourself sufficient additional time to allow "B's" offer to arrive:

You should make a telephone call to the hiring manager and explain your situation. State that you're very interested in and excited by his offer and that you feel that it is an excellent long-term option. Indicate that you understand how important the job is to the company and to him and that you understand how much thought they put into making their decision to select you as a member of the team over the time period the interview process has taken. Then indicate that this decision is very important to you as well, and that whatever decision you make is one that you'll want to live with for the long-term (i.e. your goals and theirs are the same). To be fair to yourself and the company you want to make your decision with all of your options in front of you. After all, they wouldn't want you to feel forced to make a decision to join them only to continue to interview with "B" and ultimately reject their ("A's") offer two weeks later—prior to starting. That would not be in anyone's best interest. Finally, inform them of the timing involved and set a _realistic_ date for your response. Realistic means that you have a firm date for a decision from Company "B". Make certain that "A's" hiring manager can hang up the phone with the feeling that you are seriously considering his offer—not simply using it as a bargaining chip with Company "B". Having done this, hang up and continue the process with Company "B". You'll obviously want to keep Company "B" appraised of the situation, too.

Your initial reaction to this strategy might be, "Wait a second, if I'm too honest, Company "A" will just retract their offer and I'll be left with zip, hoping Company "B" comes through!" Don't forget, I've already advised you to hold your communication until after you have received "A's" offer in writing. However, my response to this reaction is that this is highly unlikely because of a dirty little secret—a secret unknown to most candidates! Believe it or not, at this stage in the process Company "A" wants you and wants you badly. Contrary to popular mythology, it is very difficult to find a great candidate—one great enough to extend an offer. Once a company has found such a candidate and committed to them, they will do everything humanly possible to bring the candidate on board. Don't forget, too, that at this stage of the game, Company "A" has already invested a significant amount of time and energy (advertising, reviewing resumes, arranging interviews, interviewing, background checking, etc.) in the process. They do not want to have to start the process anew! You may represent their immediate, best hope of hiring an outstanding individual for this critical position! It is in Company "A's" best interest to wait even another week or two for you to decide, rather than having to start the process over again. If you properly communicate your rationale as described above, you should be able to gain the additional time you'll need to perform a true comparison; that is, Company "A's" offer vs. Company "B's".

A small point to consider, is that should you decide to accept Company "A's" offer vs. Company "B's", think of how great you've allowed "A" to feel! They have just scored a victory over the competition. As both a corporate recruiter and search consultant, I have experienced this event many times. I can assure you that this emotion is present!

If Company "A", upon hearing your proposal, decides to play hardball and not allow you the additional time to decide, then you have a decision to make. That decision is all about the proverbial "bird in the hand". However, what does this hardball approach tell you about what it would be like to work for Company "A"? Are you not gaining a snapshot of what life at Company "A" might be like? Are they not showing you an aspect of inflexibility and absolutism? Do you think this type of behavior might show itself in other ways after you've become an employee? In a sense, by rejecting your proposal, Company "A" is telling you in advance that what is in your best interest is irrelevant. Accepting "A's" offer under these conditions could have longer-term negative consequences, so I advise you to consider this sort of behavior carefully.

SHOULD YOU NEGOTIATE EVERY OFFER?

Now that the Company has committed itself and extended an offer in writing, you're probably thinking . . . "I must negotiate! They probably have 'low-balled' me. I can get more! Even if they haven't, I've been told by my friends that unless I negotiate they won't respect me!" Many times, candidates are made great offers only to feel that they have to hold out and counter the offer for the sake of a thousand dollars or an additional week of vacation.

In some cases, it *is* necessary to negotiate the offer made—particularly if you've feel the salary offer made is not competitive. In instances such as these, I am in total support of a candidate seeking to negotiate a better offer. However, my counsel is to be able to factually support your position vs. using emotional arguments (such as, "I just think I'm worth more.") Factually supporting your position will require you to do a bit of quick homework. If the issue is salary, then investigate salaries paid for comparable jobs. Web sites such as Salary.com are filled with data that can give you a benchmark of what competitive compensation should be. Additionally, your recruiter should be able to provide you with data from their database of candidates with backgrounds similar to yours and what they are earning. My message is that if you intend to negotiate an offer, it is wise to come to the table armed with data. Most large companies have fairly sophisticated compensation programs with access to extensive data. You won't catch them unprepared if you wildly start flinging numbers about. The good news is that if you're worth more and can support it, they'll bite. There is no point in their bringing you into the company at such a low salary that you become an on-going salary "issue", or become easy prey for the next company that comes along with truly competitive compensation.

However, when a candidate seeks to negotiate an offer simply for the sake of negotiating or ego gratification, I am very suspicious. Unless you're the sort of person that enjoys this sort of thing, negotiating, simply for the sake of negotiating, is foolish. Remember, the moment you "negotiate", you have made a counter-offer. Your counter-offer abrogates the company's original offer. In other words, the original offer is no longer binding and is off the table—the company can walk away from you as a candidate at any time until another offer is committed to. If you feel the need to negotiate with a company regarding your offer, just make certain you're negotiating for the right reasons. "Playing chicken" with a company may cause them to decide that they can't (or won't) enhance their original offer and go to Plan "B"—their second-choice candidate—leaving you out in the cold.

ACCEPTING YOUR OFFER!

Before you formally accept any offer, make certain the company has confirmed the terms of the offer in writing and to your satisfaction. An offer of employment is like any other business contract and to have the best chance of enforcement, the terms of the offer must be in written form. Items such as salary and bonuses, benefit coverage (and eligibility dates), stock options, review dates, job title, reporting relationships and miscellanea (such as tuition reimbursement, vacations, etc.) must be "spelled out" in writing. Accept a verbal-only offer at your own peril! You are not being a pain in the podex by insisting on an offer letter—quite the contrary, you are confirming that you are a good businessperson.

While it is permissible to verbally accept an offer not in writing, under <u>no</u> circumstances should you share your good news with co-workers or resign from your current role <u>until</u> you have received confirmation of the verbal offer (and all of the relevant conditions) in writing. I won't bore you with the truly horrific tales I've encountered over the past years involving candidates accepting verbal offers without written confirmation. Suffice to say, your goal should be to protect yourself and your family from sunspots, space aliens, misunderstandings, faulty memories or downright deviousness.

When you are ready to formally accept your offer, here's a nice little tactic that will drive your new employer wild. During your acceptance call, tell your new employer that you're excited by this opportunity and that you want to "hit the ground running" in your new role. Ask your new boss if he or she can send you materials—or even an assignment—that will help to get you up to speed even before you start. Ask if there is a team/company meeting taking place before your starting date and would your new boss like you to attend? Chances are they will prefer you to wait until you've actually started, but the message you've just sent is a very good one! This message has them thinking, "I really made a great choice in hiring this one! They are committed to me and this company already!" Doing this is exactly the right touch that separates you from the pack and places you in the ranks of high-impact candidates.

IF YOU'VE DECIDED TO REJECT THE OFFER

Rejecting a job offer is sure to create disappointment in all of the parties involved. After all, much time, energy and thought has been expended in the process of getting this far. Therefore, prior to rejecting a company's offer, it is essential that you have done your "due diligence" regarding the offer and investigated remedies for your concerns (be they compensation, job responsibilities/title, etc.). When you have exhausted all possibilities, then rejection of the offer is the only course of action left to you. However, there is a proper manner in which to reject an offer.

The guiding principal that you should follow in rejecting your offer is that "burning bridges" is not acceptable. Your rejection must be timely, professional and your rationale well articulated. The primary reason for this is that you always want to leave the door open to receive another offer from that company or, from that hiring manager should he or she join another company in the future. Here is a brief "war story" to underscore this point:

> While I was an executive recruiter in New York City, I had a candidate that was made an offer by a large investment bank for a Project Leader (information systems) role. The candidate rejected the offer on the grounds that she was already a Project Leader at her current company

and that the role would not be moving her forward career-wise. The manner in which she rejected the offer was timely (2 days after receiving the offer and after she had made her issue known to my client) and very professional. While we (candidate, client and I) were disappointed in the outcome, it was a decision I could easily support—even though it cost me a fair amount of money—because the candidate was right! Six months later, I received a telephone call out of the blue from the same hiring manager—although now, she had joined another company, a major brokerage firm. The hiring manager asked if the candidate who had rejected her offer at the bank was still available (she was) and would she consider interviewing for a "manager" role at her new company?

You can guess the final outcome. The candidate accepted an offer for an AVP (Manager) of Information Systems role at my client's new company at a much higher salary and with expanded responsibilities, and a much larger fee for me! What made this happy ending possible was the manner in which the candidate had rejected the initial offer made by my client at her previous company. The candidate used a reasoned, thoughtful and professional approach—and that behavior earned her another time at bat with that hiring manager for an even bigger role!

So how do you reject an offer?

First, you should make your rejection timely. If you have been given 5 days to make a decision and you know on day 3 that you're going to reject, don't wait until day 5 at 4:30 PM to make the call to the company. It's likely that the company has a backup candidate (their second choice) and waiting those two extra days may cause them to lose that candidate, too! From personal experience, on all sides of the equation, I can tell you that this sort of behavior is not designed to win hearts and minds.

Second, make certain that you reject the offer by personally speaking with the hiring manager. Don't attempt to dodge the bullet by leaving a voice mail or by insisting that Human Resources or your recruiter pass along your bad news! When you speak with the hiring manager, fully articulate the rationale behind your decision, thank them for the consideration shown to you as a candidate, and offer your sincere best wishes that they can complete their search in a timely manner. Finally, ask for their email address with the promise to stay in touch. Remember, that this person is already a member of your "fan club". They've made you an offer, after all! Such "members" can become invaluable networking contacts in the future! None of us can predict the future—so who is to say that at some point you might be aggressively looking for a new position as a result of a layoff or restructuring. Wouldn't it be great to have a group of instant supporters upon whom you can call? <u>Professionally</u> declining your offer will help you to retain a relationship that might be extremely valuable to you in the future.

YOU DID NOT RECEIVE AN OFFER

First, let's make sure we understand what not receiving an offer really means. It does not mean that you are unworthy or unlikable or, that your abilities were not adequate. Being rejected simply means that the company did not feel that you were the best candidate for that particular role. You might think I state this because I am trying to soothe your feelings or soften the blow. Not at all! I *know* rejection is disappointing, but the reality is that candidates are rejected for a myriad of reasons, most of which have nothing to do with competence. A quick example to drive this point home . . .

If you have had the experience of purchasing a home, you know that one will normally look at multiple properties before making a buying decision. If you've looked at ten homes prior to making a decision, it doesn't infer that 9 were terrible and 1 was great. In fact, there may have been 2 or 3 homes that were very close contenders, but on which you opted to take a pass. Maybe you couldn't quite manage the asking price in your budget, or perhaps one the contenders had only 2 ½ baths and you wanted 3 full baths; maybe your second choice was really a great home, but it was a Cape Cod and you had your heart set on a Colonial. You get the picture. This analogy plays well in describing the reasons behind candidates not receiving offers. Not receiving an offer doesn't make you a bad candidate, simply not the right candidate, at that time, for that particular role.

When you do not receive an offer from a company—even a company you really wanted to join—there are usually forces at work which will ultimately prove that not joining that company was the right decision for all parties after all. In my business, one learns to be fatalistic about such events. Having experienced many such occurrences over the years, I can truly state that when a "deal" doesn't happen, it usually works out for the best. For example, I have had candidates "lose out:" on a search only to find out 6 months later that the position was eliminated, or that the company was downsizing or restructuring or putting a salary freeze in place. Chances are, if that candidate had gone to work for that company they'd be out looking for another job!

More important than dwelling on not receiving an offer is attempting to understand why you did not receive an offer. Gaining that understanding can help you achieve success in subsequent interviews. You should be certain to ask for feedback from the company and from your recruiter, but preferably from the hiring manager directly. Be advised, though, that there are candidates, who after getting honest feedback, turned right around and filed lawsuits for either real or imagined infractions of the law. For this reason, in this litigious age, it is unlikely that you'll get any meaningful feedback from the company. No one wants to be potentially sued for telling the truth. However, you should make the attempt in any event. If you are successful in speaking with the hiring manager, then make certain to start the dialogue by stating that your goal is not to change their decision (if you become confrontational or argumentative, it will be a very short conversation!), but instead that you are only seeking to improve your ability to interview more effectively. In that context their feedback would be extremely helpful to you. Ask for guidance and then close on a positive note, asking them for their email address so that you can send a brief email of thanks to them. Thank the hiring manager for their consideration and state that you hope that you have another chance to cross paths with them in the future. Then, add that individual to your address book and make them part of your network for the future. Again, your quest for feedback may prove futile, but I do encourage you to make the attempt. I know that this is a tough thing to ask you to do—most of us aren't overjoyed by rejection—but as always, I'm looking "downstream". Your professionalism at this time may establish a valuable professional relationship for you in the future.

After taking this step, I encourage you to debrief yourself. Analyze your interview performance. Were there questions with which you had difficulty? Were there areas in your background that were problematic or just didn't "sell"? Were your expectations regarding salary or job title/level realistic? After any game, a coach will analyze his game plan and critique the performance of his athletes. The learning that is gained from such a thorough (however, painful) analysis sets the stage for the team to win in the future. That same mentality applies to the *sport* of interviewing as well. I know that the natural human reaction is for an individual to place as much distance between themselves and the disappointment of rejection. However, I encourage you to resist that reaction and thoroughly analyze and critique your performance. I feel confident that the insight you gain, properly applied, will help you prevail in the future!

POST JOB CHANGE DISSONANCE: BUYER'S REMORSE OR SITUATION NORMAL?

OK—you accepted the offer and have started your new job. Case closed, right?

Incorrect! There's one last concept that I'd like to share with you. It's the concept of Buyer's Remorse or post job change dissonance.

Wikipedia defines "Buyer's Remorse" as a condition that stems from the post-decision dissonance that arises when a person has had to make a difficult decision or choice from among two similarly appealing alternatives.

Let's put that in simple English.

Buyer's Remorse means that we human beings have the tendency to go through a period where we question the decisions we've made—and particularly, when the decision has been a difficult one.

Typically, Buyer's Remorse takes place after we've made a large purchase (e.g. home, car, etc.) or have made a major life decision (getting married, having children, etc.). But as anyone who has gone through a period of Buyer's Remorse knows, those feelings pass and, ultimately, we wind up feeling good about the decision we made and why we made it.

It shouldn't surprise you to know, then, that people often go through a similar period of doubt after they've made a job change.

When I first started in the recruiting business, I used to call the candidates whom I'd placed within the first 2-3 weeks of their new jobs—to get of sense of "how things were going". I began to see a pattern emerge. I would get feedback such as (I'm paraphrasing), "You know, the first week was great—getting to know everybody, being in this new environment, etc.—it was like the start of a new adventure. But now that I've been here a couple of weeks, I don't know if coming here was the right decision."

Needless to say, this was a concern, and got me thinking: Did I do the right thing placing him at that company? Did I miss something? And, being honest, am I going to have to refund the fee? ☺ I would always listen to the individual, take notes, and then promise to check back in a month or so.

Sure enough, when I would call the person back at the 7-8 week mark, I'd get a completely different story! You hear the person excited about their new job and with whom they were working. Net: they were now feeling very good about the decision they'd made to join their new company.

I asked myself: What's going on? Is this the same person who was doubting themselves and their decision just 6 weeks ago?

This whole phenomenon got me thinking—was this just a form of Buyer's Remorse or was there something more subtle at work here? Here's what I found: invariably, the people with the highest level of "dissonance" were high-performers—people who had been well-respected and who were considered "stars" at their previous companies.

Consider this: you were a high-performer at your previous company. You were making a contribution to the business. You knew how everything worked, and when it didn't, how to make it work. When you spoke, everyone shut up and listened. When your phone rang, it was someone asking for your counsel or help. You had friends in whom you could confide and commiserate. In short, you were the "master" of that universe.

Now, you are in a new company where everything is different. You don't yet know how things "work". You find yourself having to re-learn processes that were formerly on autopilot for you. You have not yet established the same level of credibility at your new company as you had at your previous company, and as a result, you find yourself having to explain who you are and why you're there when you meet someone new. When you offer a suggestion or thought, it's held up to scrutiny and questioning. This is a very different scenario from what you experienced with your prior company. In effect, it's like your "creditability clock" has been reset to zero. When your phone rings, it's either a wrong number or someone calling for the person who formerly owned that extension. You'd like to talk with someone about something your new boss said to you, but there's no one, yet, who you trust enough to have the conversation with. And most important, you are used to making a contribution every day and being recognized for it. And, now you're not.

Then, a month or two goes by. You've now reestablished your credibility in your new company.

You know how things work. When the phone rings, it's actually for you. You've created new friendships and have colleagues with whom you can discuss issues. And, you are now contributing and being recognized for it. In fact, you're so fully engaged with your new company that it seems like years since you worked at your previous company.

What I've just described above is "situation normal".

The first 1-2 months at a new company can hit high-performers particularly hard because the inevitable "ramp-up" period temporarily derails their sense of "mastery"—thus, creating dissonance.

It is for this reason, I stopped calling people I placed until after they had been on board with their new companies for 2-3 months. I found I got a much clearer (and positive) view of the individual's actual thoughts about their new job and company when I waited for the normal "dissonance period" to pass.

So, to anyone who is newly hired and experiencing feelings of Buyer's Remorse or "post-decision dissonance", I say, take a few months to re-establish yourself and get back into the flow. If you've utilized the methodology expressed in this book and have done your homework prior to accepting the offer, then I'm confident those feelings of doubt will disappear, and that within 90 days or so, you'll be fully engaged in your new role and company.

CONCLUSION

So, there you have it! Throughout this book I have attempted to stress the importance of approaching the interview process as professionally as you would your chosen profession—your "real" job. That is, to focus on:

- Understanding your own motivation and objectives and the motivation and objectives of others involved in the process

- Thorough preparation

- Practice, practice, practice

- Professionalism and integrity as you move throughout the process

As I indicated in the Introduction, I do not expect that everything contained within these pages to be directly applicable to you as a candidate. After all, every candidate and every situation are different and governed by an almost infinite number of variables. My goal has been to increase your awareness of the employment process. With this increased understanding, you should now be able to successfully navigate the wide range of scenarios that can confront you in your search for a new role.

Remember our gold-mining friend at the beginning of the book? I'm guessing that you had to move a ton of rock reading this book—but I'm hoping you were able to dig out at least a few nuggets of gold. Take those nuggets that apply to your own personal circumstance, use them well, and you will indeed become a *HIGH-IMPACT CANDIDATE!*

GJS Note: Getting feedback is important to me and I value yours! Please email me with your comments and reactions at:

<u>highimpactcandidate@gmail.com</u>

Made in the USA
Columbia, SC
05 September 2021